Childhood

And

Adolescence

Jacques Casanova de Seingalt

[ZHINGOORA BOOKS]

CASANOVA AT DUX

An Unpublished Chapter of History, By Arthur Symons

I

The Memoirs of Casanova, though they have enjoyed the popularity of a bad reputation, have never had justice done to them by serious students of literature, of life, and of history. One English writer, indeed, Mr. Havelock Ellis, has realised that 'there are few more delightful books in the world,' and he has analysed them in an essay on Casanova, published in Affirmations, with extreme care and remarkable subtlety. But this essay stands alone, at all events in English, as an attempt to take Casanova seriously, to show him in his relation to his time, and in his relation to human problems. And yet these Memoirs are perhaps the most valuable document which we possess on the society of the eighteenth century; they are the history of a unique life, a unique personality, one of the greatest of autobiographies; as a record of adventures, they are more entertaining than Gil Blas, or Monte Cristo, or any of the imaginary travels, and escapes, and masquerades in life, which have been written in imitation of them. They tell the story of a man who loved life passionately for its own sake: one to whom woman was, indeed, the most important thing in the world, but to whom nothing in the world was indifferent. The bust which gives us the most lively notion of him shows us a great, vivid, intellectual face, full of fiery energy and calm resource, the face of a thinker and a fighter in one. A scholar, an adventurer, perhaps a Cabalist, a busy stirrer in politics, a gamester, one 'born for the fairer sex,' as he tells us, and born also to be a vagabond; this man, who is remembered now for his written account of his own life, was that rarest kind of autobiographer, one who did not live to write, but wrote because he had lived, and when he could live no longer.

And his Memoirs take one all over Europe, giving sidelights, all the more valuable in being almost accidental, upon many of the affairs and people most interesting to us during two-thirds of the eighteenth century. Giacomo Casanova was born in Venice, of Spanish and Italian parentage, on April 2, 1725; he died at the Chateau of Dux, in Bohemia, on June 4, 1798. In that lifetime of seventy-three years he travelled, as his Memoirs show us, in Italy, France, Germany, Austria, England, Switzerland, Belgium, Russia, Poland, Spain, Holland, Turkey; he met Voltaire at Ferney, Rousseau at Montmorency, Fontenelle, d'Alembert and Crebillon at Paris, George III. in London, Louis XV. at Fontainebleau, Catherine the Great at St. Petersburg, Benedict XII. at Rome, Joseph II. at Vienna, Frederick the Great at Sans-Souci. Imprisoned by the Inquisitors of State in the Piombi at Venice, he made, in 1755, the most famous escape in history. His Memoirs, as we have them, break off abruptly at the moment when he is expecting a safe conduct, and the permission to return to Venice after twenty years' wanderings. He did return, as we know from documents in the Venetian archives; he returned as secret agent of the Inquisitors, and remained in their service from 1774 until 1782. At the end of 1782 he left Venice; and next year we find him in Paris, where, in 1784, he met Count Waldstein at the Venetian Ambassador's, and was invited by him to become his librarian at Dux. He accepted, and for the fourteen remaining years of his life lived at Dux, where he wrote his Memoirs.

Casanova died in 1798, but nothing was heard of the Memoirs (which the Prince de Ligne, in his own Memoirs, tells us that Casanova had read to him, and in which he found 'du dyamatique, de la rapidite, du comique, de la philosophie, des choses neuves, sublimes, inimitables meme') until the year 1820, when a certain Carlo Angiolini brought to the publishing house of Brockhaus, in Leipzig, a manuscript entitled Histoire de ma vie jusqu a l'an 1797, in the handwriting of Casanova. This manuscript, which I have examined at Leipzig, is written on foolscap paper, rather rough and yellow; it is written on both sides of the page, and in sheets or quires; here and there the paging shows that some pages have been omitted, and in their place are smaller sheets of thinner and whiter paper, all in Casanova's handsome, unmistakable handwriting. The manuscript is done up in twelve bundles, corresponding with the twelve volumes of the original edition; and only in one place is there a gap. The fourth and fifth chapters of the twelfth volume are missing, as the editor of the original edition points out, adding: 'It is not probable that these two chapters have been withdrawn from the manuscript of Casanova by a strange hand; everything leads us to believe that the author himself suppressed them, in the intention, no doubt, of re-writing them, but without having found time to do so.' The manuscript ends abruptly with the year 1774, and not with the year 1797, as the title would lead us to suppose.

This manuscript, in its original state, has never been printed. Herr Brockhaus, on obtaining possession of the manuscript, had it translated into German by Wilhelm Schutz, but with many omissions and alterations, and published this translation, volume by volume, from 1822 to 1828, under the title, 'Aus den Memoiren des Venetianers Jacob Casanova de Seingalt.' While the German edition was in course of publication, Herr Brockhaus employed a certain Jean Laforgue, a professor of the French language at Dresden, to revise the original manuscript, correcting Casanova's vigorous, but at times incorrect, and often somewhat Italian, French according to his own notions of elegant writing, suppressing passages which seemed too free-spoken from the point of view of morals and of politics, and altering the names of some of the persons referred to, or replacing those names by initials. This revised text was published in twelve volumes, the first two in 1826, the third and fourth in 1828, the fifth to the eighth in 1832, and the ninth to the twelfth in 1837; the first four bearing the imprint of Brockhaus at Leipzig and Ponthieu et Cie at Paris; the next four the imprint of Heideloff et Campe at Paris; and the last four nothing but 'A Bruxelles.' The volumes are all uniform, and were all really printed for the firm of Brockhaus. This, however far from representing the real text, is the only authoritative edition, and my references throughout this article will always be to this edition.

In turning over the manuscript at Leipzig, I read some of the suppressed passages, and regretted their suppression; but Herr Brockhaus, the present head of the firm, assured me that they are not really very considerable in number. The damage, however, to the vivacity of the whole narrative, by the persistent alterations of M. Laforgue, is incalculable. I compared many passages, and found scarcely three consecutive sentences untouched. Herr Brockhaus (whose courtesy I cannot sufficiently acknowledge) was kind enough to have a passage copied out for me, which I afterwards read over, and checked word by word. In this passage Casanova says, for instance: 'Elle venoit presque tous les jours lui faire une belle visite.' This is altered into: 'Cependant chaque jour Therese venait lui faire une visite.' Casanova says that some one 'avoit, comme de raison, forme le projet d'allier Dieu avec le diable.' This is made to read: 'Qui, comme de raison, avait saintement forme le projet d'allier les interets du ciel aux oeuvres de ce monde.' Casanova tells us that Therese would not commit a mortal sin 'pour devenir reine du monde;' pour une couronne,' corrects the indefatigable Laforgue. 'Il ne savoit que lui dire' becomes 'Dans cet etat de perplexite;' and so forth. It must, therefore, be realized that the Memoirs, as we have them, are only a kind of pale tracing of the vivid colours of the original.

When Casanova's Memoirs were first published, doubts were expressed as to their authenticity, first by Ugo Foscolo (in the Westminster Review, 1827), then by Querard, supposed to be an authority in regard to anonymous and pseudonymous writings, finally by Paul Lacroix, 'le bibliophile Jacob', who suggested, or rather expressed his 'certainty,' that the real author of the Memoirs was Stendhal, whose 'mind, character, ideas and style' he seemed to recognise on every page. This theory, as foolish and as unsupported as the Baconian theory of Shakespeare, has been carelessly accepted, or at all events accepted as possible, by many good scholars who have never taken the trouble to look into the matter for themselves. It was finally disproved by a series of articles of Armand Baschet, entitled 'Preuves curieuses de l'authenticite des Memoires de Jacques Casanova de Seingalt,' in 'Le Livre,' January, February, April and May, 1881; and these proofs were further corroborated by two articles of Alessandro d'Ancona, entitled 'Un Avventuriere del Secolo XVIII., in the 'Nuovo Antologia,' February 1 and August 1, 1882. Baschet had never himself seen the manuscript of the Memoirs, but he had learnt all the facts about it from Messrs. Brockhaus, and he had himself examined the numerous papers relating to Casanova in the Venetian archives. A similar examination was made at the Frari at about the same time by the Abbe Fulin; and I myself, in 1894, not knowing at the time that the discovery had been already made, made it over again for myself. There the arrest of Casanova, his imprisonment in the Piombi, the exact date of his escape, the name of the monk who accompanied him, are all authenticated by documents contained in the 'riferte' of the Inquisition of State; there are the bills for the repairs of the roof and walls of the cell from which he escaped; there are the reports of the spies on whose information he was arrested, for his too dangerous free-spokenness in matters of religion and morality. The same archives contain forty-eight letters of Casanova to the Inquisitors of State, dating from 1763 to 1782, among the Riferte dei Confidenti, or reports of secret agents; the earliest asking permission to return to Venice, the rest giving information in regard to the immoralities of the city, after his return there; all in the same handwriting as the Memoirs. Further proof could scarcely be needed, but Baschet has done more than prove the authenticity, he has proved the extraordinary veracity, of the Memoirs. F. W. Barthold, in 'Die Geschichtlichen Personlichkeiten in J. Casanova's Memoiren,' 2 vols., 1846, had already examined about a hundred of Casanova's allusions to well known people, showing the perfect exactitude of all but six or seven, and out of these six or seven inexactitudes ascribing only a single one to the author's intention. Baschet and d'Ancona both carry on what Barthold had begun; other investigators, in France, Italy and Germany, have followed them; and two things are now certain, first, that Casanova himself wrote the Memoirs published under his name, though not textually in the precise form in which we have them; and, second, that as their veracity becomes more and more evident as they are confronted with more and more independent witnesses, it is only fair to suppose that they are equally truthful where the facts are such as could only have been known to Casanova himself.

II

For more than two-thirds of a century it has been known that Casanova spent the last fourteen years of his life at Dux, that he wrote his Memoirs there, and that he died there. During all this time people have been discussing the authenticity and the truthfulness of the Memoirs, they have been searching for information about Casanova in various directions, and yet hardly any one has ever taken the trouble, or obtained the permission, to make a careful examination in precisely the one place where information was most likely to be found. The very existence of the manuscripts at Dux was known only to a few, and to most of these only on hearsay; and thus the singular good fortune was reserved for me, on my visit to Count Waldstein in September 1899, to be the first to discover the most interesting things contained in these manuscripts. M. Octave Uzanne, though he had not himself visited Dux, had indeed procured copies of some of the manuscripts, a few of which were published by him in Le Livre, in 1887 and 1889. But with the death of Le Livre in 1889 the 'Casanova inedit' came to an end, and has never, so far as I know, been continued elsewhere. Beyond the publication of these fragments, nothing has been done with the manuscripts at Dux, nor has an account of them ever been given by any one who has been allowed to examine them.

For five years, ever since I had discovered the documents in the Venetian archives, I had wanted to go to Dux; and in 1899, when I was staying with Count Lutzow at Zampach, in Bohemia, I found the way kindly opened for me. Count Waldstein, the present head of the family, with extreme courtesy, put all his manuscripts at my disposal, and invited me to stay with him. Unluckily, he was called away on the morning of the day that I reached Dux. He had left everything ready for me, and I was shown over the castle by a friend of his, Dr. Kittel, whose courtesy I should like also to acknowledge. After a hurried visit to the castle we started on the long drive to Oberleutensdorf, a smaller Schloss near Komotau, where the Waldstein family was then staying. The air was sharp and bracing; the two Russian horses flew like the wind; I was whirled along in an unfamiliar darkness, through a strange country, black with coal mines, through dark pine woods, where a wild peasantry dwelt in little mining towns. Here and there, a few men and women passed us on the road, in their Sunday finery; then a long space of silence, and we were in the open country, galloping between broad fields; and always in a haze of lovely hills, which I saw more distinctly as we drove back next morning.

The return to Dux was like a triumphal entry, as we dashed through the market-place filled with people come for the Monday market, pots and pans and vegetables strewn in heaps all over the ground, on the rough paving stones, up to the great gateway of the castle, leaving but just room for us to drive through their midst. I had the sensation of an enormous building: all Bohemian castles are big, but this one was like a royal palace. Set there in the midst of the town, after the Bohemian fashion, it opens at the back upon great gardens, as if it were in the midst of the country. I walked through room after room, along corridor after corridor; everywhere there were pictures, everywhere portraits of Wallenstein, and battle-scenes in which he led on his troops. The library, which was formed, or at least arranged, by Casanova, and which remains as he left it, contains some 25,000 volumes, some of them of considerable value; one of the most famous books in Bohemian literature, Skala's History of the Church, exists in manuscript at Dux, and it is from this manuscript that the two published volumes of it were printed. The library forms part of the Museum, which occupies a ground-floor wing of the castle. The first room is an armoury, in which all kinds of arms are arranged, in a decorative way, covering the ceiling and the walls with strange patterns. The second room contains pottery, collected by Casanova's Waldstein on his Eastern travels. The third room is full of curious mechanical toys, and cabinets, and carvings in ivory. Finally, we come to the library, contained in the two innermost rooms. The book-shelves are painted white, and reach to the low-vaulted ceilings, which are whitewashed. At the end of a bookcase, in the corner of one of the windows, hangs a fine engraved portrait of Casanova.

After I had been all over the castle, so long Casanova's home, I was taken to Count Waldstein's study, and left there with the manuscripts. I found six huge cardboard cases, large enough to contain foolscap paper, lettered on the back: 'Grafl. Waldstein-Wartenberg'sches Real Fideicommiss. Dux-Oberleutensdorf: Handschriftlicher Nachlass Casanova.' The cases were arranged so as to stand like books; they opened at the side; and on opening them, one after another, I found series after series of manuscripts roughly thrown together, after some pretence at arrangement, and lettered with a very generalised description of contents. The greater part of the manuscripts were in Casanova's handwriting, which I could see gradually beginning to get shaky with years. Most were written in French, a certain number in Italian. The beginning of a catalogue in the library, though said to be by him, was not in his handwriting. Perhaps it was taken down at his dictation. There were also some copies of Italian and Latin poems not written by him. Then there were many big bundles of letters addressed to him, dating over more than thirty years. Almost all the rest was in his own handwriting.

I came first upon the smaller manuscripts, among which I found, jumbled together on the same and on separate scraps of paper, washing-bills, accounts, hotel bills, lists of letters written, first drafts of letters with many erasures, notes on books, theological and mathematical notes, sums, Latin quotations, French and Italian verses, with variants, a long list of classical names which have and have not been 'francises,' with reasons for and against; 'what I must wear at Dresden'; headings without anything to follow, such as: 'Reflexions on respiration, on the true cause of youth-the crows'; a new method of winning the lottery at Rome; recipes, among which is a long printed list of perfumes sold at Spa; a newspaper cutting, dated Prague, 25th October 1790, on the thirty-seventh balloon ascent of Blanchard; thanks to some 'noble donor' for the gift of a dog called 'Finette'; a passport for 'Monsieur de Casanova, Venitien, allant d'ici en Hollande, October 13, 1758 (Ce Passeport bon pour quinze jours)', together with an order for post-horses, gratis, from Paris to Bordeaux and Bayonne.'

Occasionally, one gets a glimpse into his daily life at Dux, as in this note, scribbled on a fragment of paper (here and always I translate the French literally): 'I beg you to tell my servant what the biscuits are that I like to eat; dipped in wine, to fortify my stomach. I believe that they can all be found at Roman's.' Usually, however, these notes, though often suggested by something closely personal, branch off into more general considerations; or else begin with general considerations, and end with a case in point. Thus, for instance, a fragment of three pages begins: 'A compliment which is only made to gild the pill is a positive impertinence, and Monsieur Bailli is nothing but a charlatan; the monarch ought to have spit in his face, but the monarch trembled with fear.' A manuscript entitled 'Essai d'Egoisme,' dated, 'Dux, this 27th June, 1769,' contains, in the midst of various reflections, an offer to let his 'appartement' in return for enough money to 'tranquillise for six months two Jew creditors at Prague.' Another manuscript is headed 'Pride and

Folly,' and begins with a long series of antitheses, such as: 'All fools are not proud, and all proud men are fools. Many fools are happy, all proud men are unhappy.' On the same sheet follows this instance or application:

Whether it is possible to compose a Latin distich of the greatest beauty without knowing either the Latin language or prosody. We must examine the possibility and the impossibility, and afterwards see who is the man who says he is the author of the distich, for there are extraordinary people in the world. My brother, in short, ought to have composed the distich, because he says so, and because he confided it to me tete-'a-tete. I had, it is true, difficulty in believing him; but what is one to do! Either one must believe, or suppose him capable of telling a lie which could only be told by a fool; and that is impossible, for all Europe knows that my brother is not a fool.

Here, as so often in these manuscripts, we seem to see Casanova thinking on paper. He uses scraps of paper (sometimes the blank page of a letter, on the other side of which we see the address) as a kind of informal diary; and it is characteristic of him, of the man of infinitely curious mind, which this adventurer really was, that there are so few merely personal notes among these casual jottings. Often, they are purely abstract; at times, metaphysical 'jeux d'esprit,' like the sheet of fourteen 'Different Wagers,' which begins:

I wager that it is not true that a man who weighs a hundred pounds will weigh more if you kill him. I wager that if there is any difference, he will weigh less. I wager that diamond powder has not sufficient force to kill a man.

Side by side with these fanciful excursions into science, come more serious ones, as in the note on Algebra, which traces its progress since the year 1494, before which 'it had only arrived at the solution of problems of the second degree, inclusive.' A scrap of paper tells us that Casanova 'did not like regular towns.' 'I like,' he says, 'Venice, Rome, Florence, Milan, Constantinople, Genoa.' Then he becomes abstract and inquisitive again, and writes two pages, full of curious, out-of-the-way learning, on the name of Paradise:

The name of Paradise is a name in Genesis which indicates a place of pleasure (lieu voluptueux): this term is Persian. This place of pleasure was made by God before he had created man.

It may be remembered that Casanova quarrelled with Voltaire, because Voltaire had told him frankly that his translation of L'Ecossaise was a bad translation. It is piquant to read another note written in this style of righteous indignation:

Voltaire, the hardy Voltaire, whose pen is without bit or bridle; Voltaire, who devoured the Bible, and ridiculed our dogmas, doubts, and after having made proselytes to impiety, is not ashamed, being reduced to the extremity of life, to ask for the sacraments, and to cover his body with more relics than St. Louis had at Amboise.

Here is an argument more in keeping with the tone of the Memoirs:

A girl who is pretty and good, and as virtuous as you please, ought not to take it ill that a man, carried away by her charms, should set himself to the task of making their conquest. If this man cannot please her by any means, even if his passion be criminal, she ought never to take offence at it, nor treat him

14

unkindly; she ought to be gentle, and pity him, if she does not love him, and think it enough to keep invincibly hold upon her own duty.

Occasionally he touches upon aesthetical matters, as in a fragment which begins with this liberal definition of beauty:

Harmony makes beauty, says M. de S. P. (Bernardin de St. Pierre), but the definition is too short, if he thinks he has said everything. Here is mine. Remember that the subject is metaphysical. An object really beautiful ought to seem beautiful to all whose eyes fall upon it. That is all; there is nothing more to be said.

At times we have an anecdote and its commentary, perhaps jotted down for use in that latter part of the Memoirs which was never written, or which has been lost. Here is a single sheet, dated 'this 2nd September, 1791,' and headed Souvenir:

The Prince de Rosenberg said to me, as we went down stairs, that Madame de Rosenberg was dead, and asked me if the Comte de Waldstein had in the library the illustration of the Villa d'Altichiero, which the Emperor had asked for in vain at the city library of Prague, and when I answered 'yes,' he gave an equivocal laugh. A moment afterwards, he asked me if he might tell the Emperor. 'Why not, monseigneur? It is not a secret, 'Is His Majesty coming to Dux?' 'If he goes to Oberlaitensdorf (sic) he will go to Dux, too; and he may ask you for it, for there is a monument there which relates to him when he was Grand Duke.' 'In that case, His Majesty can also see my critical remarks on the Egyptian prints.'

The Emperor asked me this morning, 6th October, how I employed my time at Dux, and I told him that I was making an Italian anthology. 'You have all the Italians, then?' 'All, sire.' See what a lie leads to. If I had not lied in saying that I was making an anthology, I should not have found myself obliged to lie again in saying that we have all the Italian poets. If the Emperor comes to Dux, I shall kill myself.

'They say that this Dux is a delightful spot,' says Casanova in one of the most personal of his notes, 'and I see that it might be for many; but not for me, for what delights me in my old age is independent of the place which I inhabit. When I do not sleep I dream, and when I am tired of dreaming I blacken paper, then I read, and most often reject all that my pen has vomited.' Here we see him blackening paper, on every occasion, and for every purpose. In one bundle I found an unfinished story about Roland, and some adventure with women in a cave; then a 'Meditation on arising from sleep, 19th May 1789'; then a 'Short Reflection of a Philosopher who finds himself thinking of procuring his own death. At Dux, on getting out of bed on 13th October 1793, day dedicated to St. Lucy, memorable in my too long life.' A big budget, containing cryptograms, is headed 'Grammatical Lottery'; and there is the title-page of a treatise on The Duplication of the Hexahedron, demonstrated geometrically to all the Universities and all the Academies of Europe.' [See Charles Henry, Les Connaissances Mathimatiques de Casanova. Rome, 1883.] There are innumerable verses, French and Italian, in all stages, occasionally attaining the finality of these lines, which appear in half a dozen tentative forms:

'Sans mystere point de plaisirs,
Sans silence point de mystere.
Charme divin de mes loisirs,
Solitude! que tu mes chere!

Then there are a number of more or less complete manuscripts of some extent. There is the manuscript of the translation of Homer's 'Iliad, in ottava rima (published in Venice, 1775-8); of the 'Histoire de Venise,' of the 'Icosameron,' a curious book published in 1787, purporting to be 'translated from English,' but really an original work of Casanova; 'Philocalies sur les Sottises des Mortels,' a long manuscript never published; the sketch and beginning of 'Le Pollmarque, ou la Calomnie demasquee par la presence d'esprit. Tragicomedie en trois actes, composed a Dux dans le mois de Juin de l'Annee, 1791,' which recurs again under the form of the 'Polemoscope: La Lorgnette menteuse ou la Calomnie demasquge,' acted before the Princess de Ligne, at her chateau at Teplitz, 1791. There is a treatise in Italian, 'Delle Passioni'; there are long dialogues, such as 'Le Philosophe et le Theologien', and 'Reve': 'Dieu-Moi'; there is the 'Songe d'un Quart d'Heure', divided into minutes; there is the very lengthy criticism of 'Bernardin de Saint-Pierre'; there is the 'Confutation d'une Censure indiscrate qu'on lit dans la Gazette de Iena, 19 Juin 1789'; with another large manuscript, unfortunately imperfect, first called 'L'Insulte', and then 'Placet au Public', dated 'Dux, this 2nd March, 1790,' referring to the same criticism on the 'Icosameron' and the 'Fuite des Prisons. L'Histoire de ma Fuite des Prisons de la Republique de Venise, qu'on appelle les Plombs', which is the first draft of the most famous part of the Memoirs, was published at Leipzig in 1788; and, having read it in the Marcian Library at Venice, I am not surprised to learn from this indignant document that it was printed 'under the care of a young Swiss, who had the talent to commit a hundred faults of orthography.'

III.

We come now to the documents directly relating to the Memoirs, and among these are several attempts at a preface, in which we see the actual preface coming gradually into form. One is entitled 'Casanova au Lecteur', another 'Histoire de mon Existence', and a third Preface. There is also a brief and characteristic 'Precis de ma vie', dated November 17, 1797. Some of these have been printed in Le Livre, 1887. But by far the most important manuscript that I discovered, one which, apparently, I am the first to discover, is a manuscript entitled 'Extrait du Chapitre 4 et 5. It is written on paper similar to that on which the Memoirs are written; the pages are numbered 104-148; and though it is described as Extrait, it seems to contain, at all events, the greater part of the missing chapters to which I have already referred, Chapters IV. and V. of the last volume of the Memoirs. In this manuscript we find Armeline and Scolastica, whose story is interrupted by the abrupt ending of Chapter III.; we find Mariuccia of Vol. VII, Chapter IX., who married a hairdresser; and we find also Jaconine, whom Casanova recognises as his daughter, 'much prettier than Sophia, the daughter of Therese Pompeati, whom I had left at London.' It is curious that this very important manuscript, which supplies the one missing link in the Memoirs, should never have been discovered by any of the few people who have had the opportunity of looking over the Dux manuscripts. I am inclined to explain it by the fact that the case in which I found this manuscript contains some papers not relating to Casanova. Probably, those who looked into this case looked no further. I have told Herr Brockhaus of my discovery, and I hope to see Chapters IV. and V. in their places when the long-looked-for edition of the complete text is at length given to the world.

Another manuscript which I found tells with great piquancy the whole story of the Abbe de Brosses' ointment, the curing of the Princess de Conti's pimples, and the birth of the Duc de Montpensier, which is told very briefly, and with much less point, in the Memoirs (vol. iii., p. 327). Readers of the Memoirs will remember the duel at Warsaw with Count Branicki in 1766 (vol. X., pp. 274-320), an affair which attracted a good deal of attention at the time, and of which there is an account in a letter from the Abbe Taruffi to the dramatist, Francesco Albergati, dated Warsaw, March 19, 1766, quoted in Ernesto Masi's Life of Albergati, Bologna, 1878. A manuscript at Dux in Casanova's handwriting gives an account of this duel in the third person; it is entitled, 'Description de l'affaire arrivee a Varsovie le 5 Mars, 1766'. D'Ancona, in the Nuova Antologia (vol. lxvii., p. 412), referring to the Abbe Taruffi's account, mentions what he considers to be a slight discrepancy: that Taruffi refers to the danseuse, about whom the duel was fought, as La Casacci, while Casanova refers to her as La Catai. In this manuscript Casanova always refers to her as La Casacci; La Catai is evidently one of M. Laforgue's arbitrary alterations of the text.

In turning over another manuscript, I was caught by the name Charpillon, which every reader of the Memoirs will remember as the name of the harpy by whom Casanova suffered so much in London, in 1763-4. This manuscript begins by saying: 'I have been in London for six months and have been to see them (that is, the mother and daughter) in their own house,' where he finds nothing but 'swindlers, who cause all who go there to lose their money in gambling.' This manuscript adds some details to the story told in the ninth and tenth volumes of the Memoirs, and refers to the meeting with the Charpillons four and a half years before, described in Volume V., pages 428-485. It is written in a tone of great indignation. Elsewhere, I found a letter written by Casanova, but not signed, referring to an anonymous letter which he had received in reference to the Charpillons, and ending: 'My handwriting is known.' It was not until the last that I came upon great bundles of letters addressed to Casanova, and so carefully preserved that little scraps of paper, on which postscripts are written, are still in their places. One still sees the seals on the backs of many of the letters, on paper which has slightly yellowed with age, leaving the ink, however, almost always fresh. They come from Venice, Paris, Rome, Prague, Bayreuth, The Hague, Genoa, Fiume, Trieste, etc., and are addressed to as many places, often poste restante. Many are letters from women, some in beautiful handwriting, on thick paper; others on scraps of paper, in painful hands, ill-spelt. A Countess writes pitifully, imploring help; one protests her love, in spite of the 'many chagrins' he has caused her; another asks 'how they are to live together'; another laments that a report has gone about that she is secretly living with him, which may harm his reputation. Some are in French, more in Italian. 'Mon cher Giacometto', writes one woman, in French; 'Carissimo a Amatissimo', writes another, in Italian. These letters from women are in some confusion, and are in need of a good deal of sorting over and rearranging before their full extent can be realised. Thus I found letters in the same handwriting separated by letters in other handwritings; many are unsigned, or signed only by a single initial; many are undated, or dated only with the day of the week or month. There are a great many letters, dating from 1779 to 1786, signed 'Francesca Buschini,' a name which I cannot identify; they are written in Italian, and one of them begins: 'Unico Mio vero Amico' ('my only true friend'). Others are signed 'Virginia B.'; one of these is dated, 'Forlì, October 15, 1773.' There is also a 'Theresa B.,' who writes from Genoa. I was at first unable to identify the writer of a whole series of letters in French, very affectionate and intimate letters, usually unsigned, occasionally signed 'B.' She calls herself votre petite amie; or she ends with a half-smiling, half-reproachful 'goodnight, and sleep better than I' In one letter, sent from Paris in 1759, she writes: 'Never believe me, but when I tell you that I love you, and that I shall love you always: In another letter, ill-spelt, as her letters often are, she writes: 'Be assured that evil tongues, vapours, calumny, nothing can change my heart, which is yours entirely, and has no will to change its master.' Now, it seems to me that these letters must be from Manon Baletti, and that they are the letters referred to in the sixth volume of the Memoirs. We read there (page 60) how on Christmas Day, 1759, Casanova receives a letter from Manon in Paris, announcing her marriage with 'M. Blondel, architect to the King, and member of his Academy'; she returns him his letters, and begs him to return hers, or burn them. Instead of doing so he allows Esther to read them, intending to burn them afterwards. Esther begs to be allowed to keep the letters, promising to 'preserve them religiously all her life.' 'These letters,' he says, 'numbered more than two hundred, and the shortest were of four pages: Certainly there are not two hundred of them at Dux, but it seems to me highly probable that Casanova made a final selection from Manon's letters, and that it is these which I have found.

But, however this may be, I was fortunate enough to find the set of letters which I was most anxious to find the letters from Henriette, whose loss every writer on Casanova has lamented. Henriette, it will be remembered, makes her first appearance at Cesena, in the year 1748; after their meeting at Geneva, she reappears, romantically 'a propos', twenty-two years later, at Aix in Provence; and she writes to Casanova proposing 'un commerce epistolaire', asking him what he has done since his escape from prison, and promising to do her best to tell him all that has happened to her during the long interval. After quoting her letter, he adds: 'I replied to her, accepting the correspondence that she offered me, and telling her briefly all my vicissitudes. She related to me in turn, in some forty letters, all the history of her life. If she dies before me, I shall add these letters to these Memoirs; but to-day she is still alive, and always happy, though now old.' It has never been known what became of these letters, and why they were not added to the Memoirs. I have found a great quantity of them, some signed with her married name in full, 'Henriette de Schnetzmann,' and I am inclined to think that she survived Casanova, for one of the letters is dated Bayreuth, 1798, the year of Casanova's death. They are remarkably charming, written with a mixture of piquancy and distinction; and I will quote the characteristic beginning and end of the last letter I was able to find. It begins: 'No, it is impossible to be sulky with you!' and ends: 'If I become vicious, it is you, my Mentor, who make me so, and I cast my sins upon you. Even if I were damned I should still be your most devoted friend, Henriette de Schnetzmann.' Casanova was twenty-three when he met Henriette; now, herself an old woman, she writes to him when he is seventy-three, as if the fifty years that had passed were blotted out in the faithful affection of her memory. How many more discreet and less changing lovers have had the quality of constancy in change, to which this life-long correspondence bears witness? Does it not suggest a view of Casanova not quite the view of all the world? To me it shows the real man, who perhaps of all others best understood what Shelley meant when he said:

True love in this differs from gold or clay
That to divide is not to take away.

But, though the letters from women naturally interested me the most, they were only a certain proportion of the great mass of correspondence which I turned over. There were letters from Carlo Angiolini, who was afterwards to bring the manuscript of the Memoirs to Brockhaus; from Balbi, the monk with whom Casanova escaped from the Piombi; from the Marquis Albergati, playwright, actor, and eccentric, of whom there is some account in the Memoirs; from the Marquis Mosca, 'a distinguished man of letters whom I was anxious to see,' Casanova tells us in the same volume in which he describes his visit to the Moscas at Pesaro; from Zulian, brother of the Duchess of Fiano; from Richard Lorrain, 'bel homme, ayant de l'esprit, le ton et le gout de la bonne societe', who came to settle at Gorizia in 1773, while Casanova was there; from the Procurator Morosini, whom he speaks of in the Memoirs as his 'protector,' and as one of those through whom he obtained permission to return to Venice. His other 'protector,' the 'avogador' Zaguri, had, says Casanova, 'since the affair of the Marquis Albergati, carried on a most interesting correspondence with me'; and in fact I found a bundle of no less than a hundred and thirty-eight letters from him, dating from 1784 to 1798. Another bundle contains one hundred and seventy-two letters from Count Lamberg. In the Memoirs Casanova says, referring to his visit to Augsburg at the end of 1761:

I used to spend my evenings in a very agreeable manner at the house of Count Max de Lamberg, who resided at the court of the Prince-Bishop with the title of Grand Marshal. What particularly attached me to Count Lamberg was his literary talent. A first-rate scholar, learned to a degree, he has published several much esteemed works. I carried on an exchange of letters with him which ended only with his death four years ago in 1792.

Casanova tells us that, at his second visit to Augsburg in the early part of 1767, he 'supped with Count Lamberg two or three times a week,' during the four months he was there. It is with this year that the letters I have found begin: they end with the year of his death, 1792. In his 'Memorial d'un Mondain' Lamberg refers to Casanova as 'a man known in literature, a man of profound knowledge.' In the first edition of 1774, he laments that 'a man such as M. de S. Galt' should not yet have been taken back into favour by the Venetian government, and in the second edition, 1775, rejoices over Casanova's return to Venice. Then there are letters from Da Ponte, who tells the story of Casanova's curious relations with Mme. d'Urfe, in his 'Memorie scritte da esso', 1829; from Pittoni, Bono, and others mentioned in different parts of the Memoirs, and from some dozen others who are not mentioned in them. The only letters in the whole collection that have been published are those from the Prince de Ligne and from Count Koenig.

IV.

Casanova tells us in his Memoirs that, during his later years at Dux, he had only been able to 'hinder black melancholy from devouring his poor existence, or sending him out of his mind,' by writing ten or twelve hours a day. The copious manuscripts at Dux show us how persistently he was at work on a singular variety of subjects, in addition to the Memoirs, and to the various books which he published during those years. We see him jotting down everything that comes into his head, for his own amusement, and certainly without any thought of publication; engaging in learned controversies, writing treatises on abstruse mathematical problems, composing comedies to be acted before Count Waldstein's neighbours, practising verse-writing in two languages, indeed with more patience than success, writing philosophical dialogues in which God and himself are the speakers, and keeping up an extensive correspondence, both with distinguished men and with delightful women. His mental activity, up to the age of seventy-three, is as prodigious as the activity which he had expended in living a multiform and incalculable life. As in life everything living had interested him so in his retirement from life every idea makes its separate appeal to him; and he welcomes ideas with the same impartiality with which he had welcomed adventures. Passion has intellectualised itself, and remains not less passionate. He wishes to do everything, to compete with every one; and it is only after having spent seven years in heaping up miscellaneous learning, and exercising his faculties in many directions, that he turns to look back over his own past life, and to live it over again in memory, as he writes down the narrative of what had interested him most in it. 'I write in the hope that my history will never see the broad day light of publication,' he tells us, scarcely meaning it, we may be sure, even in the moment of hesitancy which may naturally come to him. But if ever a book was written for the pleasure of writing it, it was this one; and an autobiography written for oneself is not likely to be anything but frank.

'Truth is the only God I have ever adored,' he tells us: and we now know how truthful he was in saying so. I have only summarised in this article the most important confirmations of his exact accuracy in facts and dates; the number could be extended indefinitely. In the manuscripts we find innumerable further confirmations; and their chief value as testimony is that they tell us nothing which we should not have already known, if we had merely taken Casanova at his word. But it is not always easy to take people at their own word, when they are writing about themselves; and the world has been very loth to believe in Casanova as he represents himself. It has been specially loth to believe that he is telling the truth when he tells us about his adventures with women. But the letters contained among these manuscripts shows us the women of Casanova writing to him with all the fervour and all the fidelity which he attributes to them; and they show him to us in the character of as fervid and faithful a lover. In every fact, every detail, and in the whole mental impression which they convey, these manuscripts bring before us the Casanova of the Memoirs. As I seemed to come upon Casanova at home, it was as if I came upon old friend, already perfectly known to me, before I had made my pilgrimage to Dux.

1902

TRANSLATOR'S PREFACE

A series of adventures wilder and more fantastic than the wildest of romances, written down with the exactitude of a business diary; a view of men and cities from Naples to Berlin, from Madrid and London to Constantinople and St. Petersburg; the 'vie intime' of the eighteenth century depicted by a man, who to-day sat with cardinals and saluted crowned heads, and to morrow lurked in dens of profligacy and crime; a book of confessions penned without reticence and without penitence; a record of forty years of "occult" charlatanism; a collection of tales of successful imposture, of 'bonnes fortunes', of marvellous escapes, of transcendent audacity, told with the humour of Smollett and the delicate wit of Voltaire. Who is there interested in men and letters, and in the life of the past, who would not cry, "Where can such a book as this be found?"

Yet the above catalogue is but a brief outline, a bare and meagre summary, of the book known as "THE MEMOIRS OF CASANOVA"; a work absolutely unique in literature. He who opens these wonderful pages is as one who sits in a theatre and looks across the gloom, not on a stage-play, but on another and a vanished world. The curtain draws up, and suddenly a hundred and fifty years are rolled away, and in bright light stands out before us the whole life of the past; the gay dresses, the polished wit, the careless morals, and all the revel and dancing of those merry years before the mighty deluge of the Revolution. The palaces and marble stairs of old Venice are no longer desolate, but thronged with scarlet-robed senators, prisoners with the doom of the Ten upon their heads cross the Bridge of Sighs, at dead of night the nun slips out of the convent gate to the dark canal where a gondola is waiting, we assist at the 'parties fines' of cardinals, and we see the bank made at faro. Venice gives place to the assembly rooms of Mrs. Cornely and the fast taverns of the London of 1760; we pass from Versailles to the Winter Palace of St. Petersburg in the days of Catherine, from the policy of the Great Frederick to the lewd mirth of strolling-players, and the presence-chamber of the Vatican is succeeded by an intrigue in a garret. It is indeed a new experience to read this history of a man who, refraining from nothing, has concealed nothing; of one who stood in the courts of Louis the Magnificent before Madame de Pompadour and the nobles of the Ancien Regime, and had an affair with an adventuress of Denmark Street, Soho; who was bound over to keep the peace by Fielding, and knew Cagliostro. The friend of popes and kings and noblemen, and of all the male and female ruffians and vagabonds of Europe, abbe, soldier, charlatan, gamester, financier, diplomatist, viveur, philosopher, virtuoso, "chemist, fiddler, and buffoon," each of these, and all of these was Giacomo Casanova, Chevalier de Seingalt, Knight of the Golden Spur.

And not only are the Memoirs a literary curiosity; they are almost equally curious from a bibliographical point of view. The manuscript was written in French and came into the possession of the publisher Brockhaus, of Leipzig, who had it translated into German, and printed. From this German edition, M. Aubert de Vitry re-translated the work into French, but omitted about a fourth of the matter, and this mutilated and worthless version is frequently purchased by unwary bibliophiles. In the year 1826, however, Brockhaus, in order presumably to protect his property, printed the entire text of the original MS. in French, for the first time, and in this complete form, containing a large number of anecdotes and incidents not to be found in the spurious version, the work was not acceptable to the authorities, and was consequently rigorously suppressed. Only a few copies sent out for presentation or for review are known to have escaped, and from one of these rare copies the present translation has been made and solely for private circulation.

In conclusion, both translator and 'editeur' have done their utmost to present the English Casanova in a dress worthy of the wonderful and witty original.

AUTHOR'S PREFACE

I will begin with this confession: whatever I have done in the course of my life, whether it be good or evil, has been done freely; I am a free agent.

The doctrine of the Stoics or of any other sect as to the force of Destiny is a bubble engendered by the imagination of man, and is near akin to Atheism. I not only believe in one God, but my faith as a Christian is also grafted upon that tree of philosophy which has never spoiled anything.

I believe in the existence of an immaterial God, the Author and Master of all beings and all things, and I feel that I never had any doubt of His existence, from the fact that I have always relied upon His providence, prayed to Him in my distress, and that He has always granted my prayers. Despair brings death, but prayer does away with despair; and when a man has prayed he feels himself supported by new confidence and endowed with power to act. As to the means employed by the Sovereign Master of human beings to avert impending dangers from those who beseech His assistance, I confess that the knowledge of them is above the intelligence of man, who can but wonder and adore. Our ignorance becomes our only resource, and happy, truly happy; are those who cherish their ignorance! Therefore must we pray to God, and believe that He has granted the favour we have been praying for, even when in appearance it seems the reverse. As to the position which our body ought to assume when we address ourselves to the Creator, a line of Petrarch settles it:

'Con le ginocchia della mente inchine.'

Man is free, but his freedom ceases when he has no faith in it; and the greater power he ascribes to faith, the more he deprives himself of that power which God has given to him when He endowed him with the gift of reason. Reason is a particle of the Creator's divinity. When we use it with a spirit of humility and justice we are certain to please the Giver of that precious gift. God ceases to be God only for those who can admit the possibility of His non-existence, and that conception is in itself the most severe punishment they can suffer.

Man is free; yet we must not suppose that he is at liberty to do everything he pleases, for he becomes a slave the moment he allows his actions to be ruled by passion. The man who has sufficient power over himself to wait until his nature has recovered its even balance is the truly wise man, but such beings are seldom met with.

The reader of these Memoirs will discover that I never had any fixed aim before my eyes, and that my system, if it can be called a system, has been to glide away unconcernedly on the stream of life, trusting to the wind wherever it led. How many changes arise from such an independent mode of life! My success and my misfortunes, the bright and the dark days I have gone through, everything has proved to me that in this world, either physical or moral, good comes out of evil just as well as evil comes out of good. My errors will point to thinking men the various roads, and will teach them the great art of treading on the brink of the precipice without falling into it. It is only necessary to have courage, for strength without self-confidence is useless. I have often met with happiness after some imprudent step which ought to have brought ruin upon me, and although passing a vote of censure upon myself I would thank God for his mercy. But, by way of compensation, dire misfortune has befallen me in consequence of actions prompted by the most cautious wisdom. This would humble me; yet conscious that I had acted rightly I would easily derive comfort from that conviction.

In spite of a good foundation of sound morals, the natural offspring of the Divine principles which had been early rooted in my heart, I have been throughout my life the victim of my senses; I have found delight in losing the right path, I have constantly lived in the midst of error, with no consolation but the consciousness of my being mistaken. Therefore, dear reader, I trust that, far from attaching to my history the character of impudent boasting, you will find in my Memoirs only the characteristic proper to a general confession, and that my narratory style will be the manner neither of a repenting sinner, nor of a man ashamed to acknowledge his frolics. They are the follies inherent to youth; I make sport of them, and, if you are kind, you will not yourself refuse them a good-natured smile. You will be amused when you see that I have more than once deceived without the slightest qualm of conscience, both knaves and fools. As to the deceit perpetrated upon women, let it pass, for, when love is in the way, men and women as a general rule dupe each other. But on the score of fools it is a very different matter. I always feel the greatest bliss when I recollect those I have caught in my snares, for they generally are insolent, and so self-conceited that they challenge wit. We avenge intellect when we dupe a fool, and it is a victory not to be despised for a fool is covered with steel and it is often very hard to find his vulnerable part. In fact, to gull a fool seems to me an exploit worthy of a witty man. I have felt in my very blood, ever since I was born, a most unconquerable hatred towards the whole tribe of fools, and it arises from the fact that I feel myself a blockhead whenever I am in their company. I am very far from placing them in the same class with those men whom we call stupid, for the latter are stupid only from deficient education, and I rather like them. I have met with some of them—very honest fellows, who, with all their stupidity, had a kind of intelligence and an upright good sense, which cannot be the characteristics of fools. They are like eyes veiled with the cataract, which, if the disease could be removed, would be very beautiful.

Dear reader, examine the spirit of this preface, and you will at once guess at my purpose. I have written a preface because I wish you to know me thoroughly before you begin the reading of my Memoirs. It is only in a coffee-room or at a table d'hote that we like to converse with strangers.

I have written the history of my life, and I have a perfect right to do so; but am I wise in throwing it before a public of which I know nothing but evil? No, I am aware it is sheer folly, but I want to be busy, I want to laugh, and why should I deny myself this gratification?

'Expulit elleboro morbum bilemque mero.'

An ancient author tells us somewhere, with the tone of a pedagogue, if you have not done anything worthy of being recorded, at least write something worthy of being read. It is a precept as beautiful as a diamond of the first water cut in England, but it cannot be applied to me, because I have not written either a novel, or the life of an illustrious character. Worthy or not, my life is my subject, and my subject is my life. I have lived without dreaming that I should ever take a fancy to write the history of my life, and, for that very reason, my Memoirs may claim from the reader an interest and a sympathy which they would not have obtained, had I always entertained the design to write them in my old age, and, still more, to publish them.

I have reached, in 1797, the age of three-score years and twelve; I can not say, Vixi, and I could not procure a more agreeable pastime than to relate my own adventures, and to cause pleasant laughter amongst the good company listening to me, from which I have received so many tokens of friendship, and in the midst of which I have ever lived. To enable me to write well, I have only to think that my readers will belong to that polite society:

'Quoecunque dixi, si placuerint, dictavit auditor.'

Should there be a few intruders whom I can not prevent from perusing my Memoirs, I must find comfort in the idea that my history was not written for them.

By recollecting the pleasures I have had formerly, I renew them, I enjoy them a second time, while I laugh at the remembrance of troubles now past, and which I no longer feel. A member of this great universe, I speak to the air, and I fancy myself rendering an account of my administration, as a steward is wont to do before leaving his situation. For my future I have no concern, and as a true philosopher, I never would have any, for I know not what it may be: as a Christian, on the other hand, faith must believe without discussion, and the stronger it is, the more it keeps silent. I know that I have lived because I have felt, and, feeling giving me the knowledge of my existence, I know likewise that I shall exist no more when I shall have ceased to feel.

Should I perchance still feel after my death, I would no longer have any doubt, but I would most certainly give the lie to anyone asserting before me that I was dead.

The history of my life must begin by the earliest circumstance which my memory can evoke; it will therefore commence when I had attained the age of eight years and four months. Before that time, if to think is to live be a true axiom, I did not live, I could only lay claim to a state of vegetation. The mind of a human being is formed only of comparisons made in order to examine analogies, and therefore cannot precede the existence of memory. The mnemonic organ was developed in my head only eight years and four months after my birth; it is then that my soul began to be susceptible of receiving impressions. How is it possible for an immaterial substance, which can neither touch nor be touched to receive impressions? It is a mystery which man cannot unravel.

A certain philosophy, full of consolation, and in perfect accord with religion, pretends that the state of dependence in which the soul stands in relation to the senses and to the organs, is only incidental and transient, and that it will reach a condition of freedom and happiness when the death of the body shall have delivered it from that state of tyrannic subjection. This is very fine, but, apart from religion, where is the proof of it all? Therefore, as I cannot, from my own information, have a perfect certainty of my being immortal until the dissolution of my body has actually taken place, people must kindly bear with me, if I am in no hurry to obtain that certain knowledge, for, in my estimation, a knowledge to be gained at the cost of life is a rather expensive piece of information. In the mean time I worship God, laying every wrong action under an interdict which I endeavour to respect, and I loathe the wicked without doing them any injury. I only abstain from doing them any good, in the full belief that we ought not to cherish serpents.

As I must likewise say a few words respecting my nature and my temperament, I premise that the most indulgent of my readers is not likely to be the most dishonest or the least gifted with intelligence.

I have had in turn every temperament; phlegmatic in my infancy; sanguine in my youth; later on, bilious; and now I have a disposition which engenders melancholy, and most likely will never change. I always made my food congenial to my constitution, and my health was always excellent. I learned very early that our health is always impaired by some excess either of food or abstinence, and I never had any physician except myself. I am bound to add that the excess in too little has ever proved in me more dangerous than the excess in too much; the last may cause indigestion, but the first causes death.

Now, old as I am, and although enjoying good digestive organs, I must have only one meal every day; but I find a set-off to that privation in my delightful sleep, and in the ease which I experience in writing down my thoughts without having recourse to paradox or sophism, which would be calculated to deceive myself even more than my readers, for I never could make up my mind to palm counterfeit coin upon them if I knew it to be such.

The sanguine temperament rendered me very sensible to the attractions of voluptuousness: I was always cheerful and ever ready to pass from one enjoyment to another, and I was at the same time very skillful in inventing new pleasures. Thence, I suppose, my natural disposition to make fresh acquaintances, and to break with them so readily, although always for a good reason, and never through mere fickleness. The errors caused by temperament are not to be corrected, because our temperament is perfectly independent of our strength: it is not the case with our character. Heart and head are the constituent parts of character; temperament has almost nothing to do with it, and, therefore, character is dependent upon education, and is susceptible of being corrected and improved.

I leave to others the decision as to the good or evil tendencies of my character, but such as it is it shines upon my countenance, and there it can easily be detected by any physiognomist. It is only on the fact that character can be read; there it lies exposed to the view. It is worthy of remark that men who have no peculiar cast of countenance, and there are a great many such men, are likewise totally deficient in peculiar characteristics, and we may establish the rule that the varieties in physiognomy are equal to the differences in character. I am aware that throughout my life my actions have received their impulse more from the force of feeling than from the wisdom of reason, and this has led me to acknowledge that my conduct has been dependent upon my nature more than upon my mind; both are generally at war, and in the midst of their continual collisions I have never found in me sufficient mind to balance my nature, or enough strength in my nature to counteract the power of my mind. But enough of this, for there is truth in the old saying: 'Si brevis esse volo, obscurus fio', and I believe that, without offending against modesty, I can apply to myself the following words of my dear Virgil:

'Nec sum adeo informis: nuper me in littore vidi
   Cum placidum ventis staret mare.'

The chief business of my life has always been to indulge my senses; I never knew anything of greater importance. I felt myself born for the fair sex, I have ever loved it dearly, and I have been loved by it as often and as much as I could. I have likewise always had a great weakness for good living, and I ever felt passionately fond of every object which excited my curiosity.

I have had friends who have acted kindly towards me, and it has been my good fortune to have it in my power to give them substantial proofs of my gratitude. I have had also bitter enemies who have persecuted me, and whom I have not crushed simply because I could not do it. I never would have forgiven them, had I not lost the memory of all the injuries they had heaped upon me. The man who forgets does not forgive, he only loses the remembrance of the harm inflicted on him; forgiveness is the offspring of a feeling of heroism, of a noble heart, of a generous mind, whilst forgetfulness is only the result of a weak memory, or of an easy carelessness, and still oftener of a natural desire for calm and quietness. Hatred, in the course of time, kills the unhappy wretch who delights in nursing it in his bosom.

Should anyone bring against me an accusation of sensuality he would be wrong, for all the fierceness of my senses never caused me to neglect any of my duties. For the same excellent reason, the accusation of drunkenness ought not to have been brought against Homer:

'Laudibus arguitur vini vinosus Homerus.'

I have always been fond of highly-seasoned, rich dishes, such as macaroni prepared by a skilful Neapolitan cook, the olla-podrida of the Spaniards, the glutinous codfish from Newfoundland, game with a strong flavour, and cheese the perfect state of which is attained when the tiny animaculae formed from its very essence begin to shew signs of life. As for women, I have always found the odour of my beloved ones exceeding pleasant.

What depraved tastes! some people will exclaim. Are you not ashamed to confess such inclinations without blushing! Dear critics, you make me laugh heartily. Thanks to my coarse tastes, I believe myself happier than other men, because I am convinced that they enhance my enjoyment. Happy are those who know how to obtain pleasures without injury to anyone; insane are those who fancy that the Almighty can enjoy the sufferings, the pains, the fasts and abstinences which they offer to Him as a sacrifice, and that His love is granted only to those who tax themselves so foolishly. God can only demand from His creatures the practice of virtues the seed of which He has sown in their soul, and all He has given unto us has been intended for our happiness; self-love, thirst for praise, emulation, strength, courage, and a power of which nothing can deprive us—the power of self-destruction, if, after due calculation, whether false or just, we unfortunately reckon death to be advantageous. This is the strongest proof of our moral freedom so much attacked by sophists. Yet this power of self-destruction is repugnant to nature, and has been rightly opposed by every religion.

A so-called free-thinker told me at one time that I could not consider myself a philosopher if I placed any faith in revelation. But when we accept it readily in physics, why should we reject it in religious matters? The form alone is the point in question. The spirit speaks to the spirit, and not to the ears. The principles of everything we are acquainted with must necessarily have been revealed to those from whom we have received them by the great, supreme principle, which contains them all. The bee erecting its hive, the swallow building its nest, the ant constructing its cave, and the spider warping its web, would never have done anything but for a previous and everlasting revelation. We must either believe that it is so, or admit that matter is endowed with thought. But as we dare not pay such a compliment to matter, let us stand by revelation.

The great philosopher, who having deeply studied nature, thought he had found the truth because he acknowledged nature as God, died too soon. Had he lived a little while longer, he would have gone much farther, and yet his journey would have been but a short one, for finding himself in his Author, he could not have denied Him: In Him we move and have our being. He would have found Him inscrutable, and thus would have ended his journey.

God, great principle of all minor principles, God, who is Himself without a principle, could not conceive Himself, if, in order to do it, He required to know His own principle.

Oh, blissful ignorance! Spinosa, the virtuous Spinosa, died before he could possess it. He would have died a learned man and with a right to the reward his virtue deserved, if he had only supposed his soul to be immortal!

It is not true that a wish for reward is unworthy of real virtue, and throws a blemish upon its purity. Such a pretension, on the contrary, helps to sustain virtue, man being himself too weak to consent to be virtuous only for his own 'gratification. I hold as a myth that Amphiaraus who preferred to be good than to seem good. In fact, I do not believe there is an honest man alive without some pretension, and here is mine.

I pretend to the friendship, to the esteem, to the gratitude of my readers. I claim their gratitude, if my Memoirs can give them instruction and pleasure; I claim their esteem if, rendering me justice, they find more good qualities in me than faults, and I claim their friendship as soon as they deem me worthy of it by the candour and the good faith with which I abandon myself to their judgment, without disguise and exactly as I am in reality. They will find that I have always had such sincere love for truth, that I have often begun by telling stories for the purpose of getting truth to enter the heads of those who could not appreciate its charms. They will not form a wrong opinion of me when they see one emptying the purse of my friends to satisfy my fancies, for those friends entertained idle schemes, and by giving them the hope of success I trusted to disappointment to cure them. I would deceive them to make them wiser, and I did not consider myself guilty, for I applied to my own enjoyment sums of money which would have been lost in the vain pursuit of possessions denied by nature; therefore I was not actuated by any avaricious rapacity. I might think myself guilty if I were rich now, but I have nothing. I have squandered everything; it is my comfort and my justification. The money was intended for extravagant follies, and by applying it to my own frolics I did not turn it into a very different, channel.

If I were deceived in my hope to please, I candidly confess I would regret it, but not sufficiently so to repent having written my Memoirs, for, after all, writing them has given me pleasure. Oh, cruel ennui! It must be by mistake that those who have invented the torments of hell have forgotten to ascribe thee the first place among them. Yet I am bound to own that I entertain a great fear of hisses; it is too natural a fear for me to boast of being insensible to them, and I cannot find any solace in the idea that, when these Memoirs are published, I shall be no more. I cannot think without a shudder of contracting any obligation towards death: I hate death; for, happy or miserable, life is the only blessing which man possesses, and those who do not love it are unworthy of it. If we prefer honour to life, it is because life is blighted by infamy; and if, in the alternative, man sometimes throws away his life, philosophy must remain silent.

Oh, death, cruel death! Fatal law which nature necessarily rejects because thy very office is to destroy nature! Cicero says that death frees us from all pains and sorrows, but this great philosopher books all the expense without taking the receipts into account. I do not recollect if, when he wrote his 'Tusculan Disputations', his own

Tullia was dead. Death is a monster which turns away from the great theatre an attentive hearer before the end of the play which deeply interests him, and this is reason enough to hate it.

All my adventures are not to be found in these Memoirs; I have left out those which might have offended the persons who have played a sorry part therein. In spite of this reserve, my readers will perhaps often think me indiscreet, and I am sorry for it. Should I perchance become wiser before I give up the ghost, I might burn every one of these sheets, but now I have not courage enough to do it.

It may be that certain love scenes will be considered too explicit, but let no one blame me, unless it be for lack of skill, for I ought not to be scolded because, in my old age, I can find no other enjoyment but that which recollections of the past afford to me. After all, virtuous and prudish readers are at liberty to skip over any offensive pictures, and I think it my duty to give them this piece of advice; so much the worse for those who may not read my preface; it is no fault of mine if they do not, for everyone ought to know that a preface is to a book what the play-bill is to a comedy; both must be read.

My Memoirs are not written for young persons who, in order to avoid false steps and slippery roads, ought to spend their youth in blissful ignorance, but for those who, having thorough experience of life, are no longer exposed to temptation, and who, having but too often gone through the fire, are like salamanders, and can be scorched by it no more. True virtue is but a habit, and I have no hesitation in saying that the really virtuous are those persons who can practice virtue without the slightest trouble; such persons are always full of toleration, and it is to them that my Memoirs are addressed.

I have written in French, and not in Italian, because the French language is more universal than mine, and the purists, who may criticise in my style some Italian turns will be quite right, but only in case it should prevent them from understanding me clearly. The Greeks admired Theophrastus in spite of his Eresian style, and the Romans delighted in their Livy in spite of his Patavinity. Provided I amuse my readers, it seems to me that I can claim the same indulgence. After all, every Italian reads Algarotti with pleasure, although his works are full of French idioms.

There is one thing worthy of notice: of all the living languages belonging to the republic of letters, the French tongue is the only one which has been condemned by its masters never to borrow in order to become richer, whilst all other languages, although richer in words than the French, plunder from it words and constructions of sentences, whenever they find that by such robbery they add something to their own beauty. Yet those who borrow the most from the French, are the most forward in trumpeting the poverty of that language, very likely thinking that such an accusation justifies their depredations. It is said that the French language has attained the apogee of its beauty, and that the smallest foreign loan would spoil it, but I make bold to assert that this is prejudice, for, although it certainly is the most clear, the most logical of all languages, it would be great temerity to affirm that it can never go farther or higher than it has gone. We all recollect that, in the days of Lulli, there was but one opinion of his music, yet Rameau came and everything was changed. The new impulse given to the French nation may open new and unexpected horizons, and new beauties, fresh perfections, may spring up from new combinations and from new wants.

The motto I have adopted justifies my digressions, and all the commentaries, perhaps too numerous, in which I indulge upon my various exploits: 'Nequidquam sapit qui sibi non sapit'. For the same reason I have always felt a great desire to receive praise and applause from polite society:

'Excitat auditor stadium, laudataque virtus
Crescit, et immensum gloria calcar habet.

I would willingly have displayed here the proud axiom: 'Nemo laeditur nisi a se ipso', had I not feared to offend the immense number of persons who, whenever anything goes wrong with them, are wont to exclaim, "It is no fault of mine!" I cannot deprive them of that small particle of comfort, for, were it not for it, they would soon feel hatred for themselves, and self-hatred often leads to the fatal idea of self-destruction.

As for myself I always willingly acknowledge my own self as the principal cause of every good or of every evil which may befall me; therefore I have always found myself capable of being my own pupil, and ready to love my teacher.

THE MEMOIRS OF JACQUES CASANOVA

CHAPTER I

My Family Pedigree—My Childhood

Don Jacob Casanova, the illegitimate son of Don Francisco Casanova, was a native of Saragosa, the capital of Aragon, and in the year of 1428 he carried off Dona Anna Palofax from her convent, on the day after she had taken the veil. He was secretary to King Alfonso. He ran away with her to Rome, where, after one year of imprisonment, the pope, Martin III., released Anna from her vows, and gave them the nuptial blessing at the instance of Don Juan Casanova, majordomo of the Vatican, and uncle of Don Jacob. All the children born from that marriage died in their infancy, with the exception of Don Juan, who, in 1475, married Donna Eleonora Albini, by whom he had a son, Marco Antonio.

In 1481, Don Juan, having killed an officer of the king of Naples, was compelled to leave Rome, and escaped to Como with his wife and his son; but having left that city to seek his fortune, he died while traveling with Christopher Columbus in the year 1493.

Marco Antonio became a noted poet of the school of Martial, and was secretary to Cardinal Pompeo Colonna.

The satire against Giulio de Medicis, which we find in his works, having made it necessary for him to leave Rome, he returned to Como, where he married Abondia Rezzonica. The same Giulio de Medicis, having become pope under the name of Clement VII, pardoned him and called him back to Rome with his wife. The city having been taken and ransacked by the Imperialists in 1526, Marco Antonio died there from an attack of the plague; otherwise he would have died of misery, the soldiers of Charles V. having taken all he possessed. Pierre Valerien speaks of him in his work 'de infelicitate litteratorum'.

Three months after his death, his wife gave birth to Jacques Casanova, who died in France at a great age, colonel in the army commanded by Farnese against Henri, king of Navarre, afterwards king of France. He had left in the city of Parma a son who married Theresa Conti, from whom he had Jacques, who, in the year 1681, married Anna Roli. Jacques had two sons, Jean-Baptiste and Gaetan-Joseph-Jacques. The eldest left Parma in 1712, and was never heard of; the other also went away in 1715, being only nineteen years old.

This is all I have found in my father's diary: from my mother's lips I have heard the following particulars:

Gaetan-Joseph-Jacques left his family, madly in love with an actress named Fragoletta, who performed the chambermaids. In his poverty, he determined to earn a living by making the most of his own person. At first he gave himself up to dancing, and five years afterwards became an actor, making himself conspicuous by his conduct still more than by his talent.

Whether from fickleness or from jealousy, he abandoned the Fragoletta, and joined in Venice a troop of comedians then giving performances at the Saint-Samuel Theatre. Opposite the house in which he had taken his lodging resided a shoemaker, by name Jerome Farusi, with his wife Marzia, and Zanetta, their only daughter—a perfect beauty sixteen years of age. The young actor fell in love with this girl, succeeded in gaining her affection, and in obtaining her consent to a runaway match. It was the only way to win her, for, being an actor, he never could have had Marzia's consent, still less Jerome's, as in their eyes a player was a most awful individual. The young lovers, provided with the necessary certificates and accompanied by two witnesses, presented themselves before the Patriarch of Venice, who performed over them the marriage ceremony. Marzia, Zanetta's mother, indulged in a good deal of exclamation, and the father died broken-hearted.

I was born nine months afterwards, on the 2nd of April, 1725.

The following April my mother left me under the care of her own mother, who had forgiven her as soon as she had heard that my father had promised never to compel her to appear on the stage. This is a promise which all actors make to the young girls they marry, and which they never fulfil, simply because their wives never care much about claiming from them the performance of it. Moreover, it turned out a very fortunate thing for my mother that she had studied for the stage, for nine years later, having been left a widow with six children, she could not have brought them up if it had not been for the resources she found in that profession.

I was only one year old when my father left me to go to London, where he had an engagement. It was in that great city that my mother made her first appearance on the stage, and in that city likewise that she gave birth to my brother Francois, a celebrated painter of battles, now residing in Vienna, where he has followed his profession since 1783.

Towards the end of the year 1728 my mother returned to Venice with her husband, and as she had become an actress she continued her artistic life. In 1730 she was delivered of my brother Jean, who became Director of the Academy of painting at Dresden, and died there in 1795; and during the three following years she became the mother of two daughters, one of whom died at an early age, while the other married in Dresden, where she still lived in 1798. I had also a posthumous brother, who became a priest; he died in Rome fifteen years ago.

Let us now come to the dawn of my existence in the character of a thinking being.

The organ of memory began to develop itself in me at the beginning of August, 1733. I had at that time reached the age of eight years and four months. Of what may have happened to me before that period I have not the faintest recollection. This is the circumstance.

I was standing in the corner of a room bending towards the wall, supporting my head, and my eyes fixed upon a stream of blood flowing from my nose to the ground. My grandmother, Marzia, whose pet I was, came to me, bathed my face with cold water, and, unknown to everyone in the house, took me with her in a gondola as far as Muran, a thickly-populated island only half a league distant from Venice.

Alighting from the gondola, we enter a wretched hole, where we find an old woman sitting on a rickety bed, holding a black cat in her arms, with five or six more purring around her. The two old cronies held together a long discourse of which, most likely, I was the subject. At the end of the dialogue, which was carried on in the patois of Forli, the witch having received a silver ducat from my grandmother, opened a box, took me in her arms, placed me in the box and locked me in it, telling me not to be frightened—a piece of advice which would certainly have had the contrary effect, if I had had any wits about me, but I was stupefied. I kept myself quiet in a corner of the box, holding a handkerchief to my nose because it was still bleeding, and otherwise very indifferent to the uproar going on outside. I could hear in turn, laughter, weeping, singing, screams, shrieks, and knocking against the box, but for all that I cared nought. At last I am taken out of the box; the blood stops flowing. The wonderful old witch, after lavishing caresses upon me, takes off my clothes, lays me on the bed, burns some drugs, gathers the smoke in a sheet which she wraps around me, pronounces incantations, takes the sheet off me, and gives me five sugar-plums of a very agreeable taste. Then she immediately rubs my temples and the nape of my neck with an ointment exhaling a delightful perfume, and puts my clothes on me again. She told me that my haemorrhage would little by little leave me, provided I should never disclose to any one what she had done to cure me, and she threatened me, on the other hand, with the loss of all my blood and with death, should I ever breathe a word concerning those mysteries. After having thus taught me my lesson, she informed me that a beautiful lady would pay me a visit during the following night, and that she would make me happy, on condition that I should have sufficient control over myself never to mention to anyone my having received such a visit. Upon this we left and returned home.

I fell asleep almost as soon as I was in bed, without giving a thought to the beautiful visitor I was to receive; but, waking up a few hours afterwards, I saw, or fancied I saw, coming down the chimney, a dazzling woman, with immense hoops, splendidly attired, and wearing on her head a crown set with precious stones, which seemed to me sparkling with fire. With slow steps, but with a majestic and sweet countenance, she came forward and sat on my bed; then taking several small boxes from her pocket, she emptied their contents over my head, softly whispering a few words, and after giving utterance to a long speech, not a single word of which I understood, she kissed me and disappeared the same way she had come. I soon went again to sleep.

The next morning, my grandmother came to dress me, and the moment she was near my bed, she cautioned me to be silent, threatening me with death if I dared to say anything respecting my night's adventures. This command, laid upon me by the only woman who had complete authority over me, and whose orders I was accustomed to obey blindly, caused me to remember the vision, and to store it, with the seal of secrecy, in the inmost corner of my dawning memory. I had not, however, the slightest inclination to mention the circumstances to anyone; in the first place, because I did not suppose it would interest anybody, and in the second because I would not have known whom to make a confidant of. My disease had rendered me dull and retired; everybody pitied me and left me to myself; my life was considered likely to be but a short one, and as to my parents, they never spoke to me.

After the journey to Muran, and the nocturnal visit of the fairy, I continued to have bleeding at the nose, but less from day to day, and my memory slowly developed itself. I learned to read in less than a month.

It would be ridiculous, of course, to attribute this cure to such follies, but at the same time I think it would be wrong to assert that they did not in any way contribute to it. As far as the apparition of the beautiful queen is concerned, I have always deemed it to be a dream, unless it should have been some masquerade got up for the occasion, but it is not always in the druggist's shop that are found the best remedies for severe diseases. Our ignorance is every day proved by some wonderful phenomenon, and I believe this to be the reason why it is so difficult to meet with a learned man entirely untainted with superstition. We know, as a matter of course, that there never have been any sorcerers in this world, yet it is true that their power has always existed in the estimation of those to whom crafty knaves have passed themselves off as such. 'Somnio nocturnos lemures portentaque Thessalia vides'.

Many things become real which, at first, had no existence but in our imagination, and, as a natural consequence, many facts which have been attributed to Faith may not always have been miraculous, although they are true miracles for those who lend to Faith a boundless power.

The next circumstance of any importance to myself which I recollect happened three months after my trip to Muran, and six weeks before my father's death. I give it to my readers only to convey some idea of the manner in which my nature was expanding.

One day, about the middle of November, I was with my brother Francois, two years younger than I, in my father's room, watching him attentively as he was working at optics. A large lump of crystal, round and cut into facets, attracted my attention. I took it up, and having brought it near my eyes I was delighted to see that it multiplied objects. The wish to possess myself of it at once got hold of me, and seeing myself unobserved I took my opportunity and hid it in my pocket.

A few minutes after this my father looked about for his crystal, and unable to find it, he concluded that one of us must have taken it. My brother asserted that he had not touched it, and I, although guilty, said the same; but my father, satisfied that he could not be mistaken, threatened to search us and to thrash the one who had told him a story. I pretended to look for the crystal in every corner of the room, and, watching my opportunity I slyly slipped it in the pocket of my brother's jacket. At first I was sorry for what I had done, for I might as well have feigned to find the crystal somewhere about the room; but the evil deed was past recall. My father, seeing that we were looking in vain, lost patience, searched us, found the unlucky ball of crystal in the pocket of the innocent boy, and inflicted upon him the promised thrashing. Three or four years later I was foolish enough to boast before my brother of the trick I had then played on him; he never forgave me, and has never failed to take his revenge whenever the opportunity offered.

However, having at a later period gone to confession, and accused myself to the priest of the sin with every circumstance surrounding it, I gained some knowledge which afforded me great satisfaction. My confessor, who was a Jesuit, told me that by that deed I had verified the meaning of my first name, Jacques, which, he said, meant, in Hebrew, "supplanter," and that God had changed for that reason the name of the ancient patriarch into that of Israel, which meant "knowing." He had deceived his brother Esau.

Six weeks after the above adventure my father was attacked with an abscess in the head which carried him off in a week. Dr. Zambelli first gave him oppilative remedies, and, seeing his mistake, he tried to mend it by administering castoreum, which sent his patient into convulsions and killed him. The abscess broke out through the ear one minute after his death, taking its leave after killing him, as if it had no longer any business with him. My father departed this life in the very prime of his manhood. He was only thirty-six years of age, but he was followed to his grave by the regrets of the public, and more particularly of all the patricians amongst whom he was held as above his profession, not less on account of his gentlemanly behaviour than on account of his extensive knowledge in mechanics.

Two days before his death, feeling that his end was at hand, my father expressed a wish to see us all around his bed, in the presence of his wife and of the Messieurs Grimani, three Venetian noblemen whose protection he wished to entreat in our favour. After giving us his blessing, he requested our mother, who was drowned in tears, to give her sacred promise that she would not educate any of us for the stage, on which he never would have appeared himself had he not been led to it by an unfortunate attachment. My mother gave her promise, and the three noblemen said that they would see to its being faithfully kept. Circumstances helped our mother to fulfill her word.

At that time my mother had been pregnant for six months, and she was allowed to remain away from the stage until after Easter. Beautiful and young as she was, she declined all the offers of marriage which were made to her, and, placing her trust in Providence, she courageously devoted herself to the task of bringing up her young family.

She considered it a duty to think of me before the others, not so much from a feeling of preference as in consequence of my disease, which had such an effect upon me that it was difficult to know what to do with me. I was very weak, without any appetite, unable to apply myself to anything, and I had all the appearance of an idiot. Physicians disagreed as to the cause of the disease. He loses, they would say, two pounds of blood every week; yet there cannot be more than sixteen or eighteen pounds in his body. What, then, can cause so abundant a bleeding? One asserted that in me all the chyle turned into blood; another was of opinion that the air I was breathing must, at each inhalation, increase the quantity of blood in my lungs, and contended that this was the reason for which I always kept my mouth open. I heard of it all six years afterward from M. Baffo, a great friend of my late father.

This M. Baffo consulted the celebrated Doctor Macop, of Padua, who sent him his opinion by writing. This consultation, which I have still in my possession, says that our blood is an elastic fluid which is liable to diminish or to increase in thickness, but never in quantity, and that my haemorrhage could only proceed from the thickness of the mass of my blood, which relieved itself in a natural way in order to facilitate circulation. The doctor added that I would have died long before, had not nature, in its wish for life, assisted itself, and he concluded by stating that the cause of the thickness of my blood could only be ascribed to the air I was breathing and that consequently I must have a change of air, or every hope of cure be abandoned. He thought likewise, that the stupidity so apparent on my countenance was caused by nothing else but the thickness of my blood.

M. Baffo, a man of sublime genius, a most lascivious, yet a great and original poet, was therefore instrumental in bringing about the decision which was then taken to send me to Padua, and to him I am indebted for my life. He died twenty years after, the last of his ancient patrician family, but his poems, although obscene, will give everlasting fame to his name. The state-inquisitors of Venice have contributed to his celebrity by their mistaken strictness. Their persecutions caused his manuscript works to become precious. They ought to have been aware that despised things are forgotten.

As soon as the verdict given by Professor Macop had been approved of, the Abbe Grimani undertook to find a good boarding-house in

Padua for me, through a chemist of his acquaintance who resided in that city. His name was Ottaviani, and he was also an antiquarian of some repute. In a few days the boarding-house was found, and on the 2nd day of April, 1734, on the very day I had accomplished my ninth year, I was taken to Padua in a 'burchiello', along the Brenta Canal. We embarked at ten o'clock in the evening, immediately after supper.

The 'burchiello' may be considered a small floating house. There is a large saloon with a smaller cabin at each end, and rooms for servants fore and aft. It is a long square with a roof, and cut on each side by glazed windows with shutters. The voyage takes eight hours. M. Grimani, M. Baffo, and my mother accompanied me. I slept with her in the saloon, and the two friends passed the night in one of the cabins. My mother rose at day break, opened one of the windows facing the bed, and the rays of the rising sun, falling on my eyes, caused me to open them. The bed was too low for me to see the land; I could see through the window only the tops of the trees along the river. The boat was sailing with such an even movement that I could not realize the fact of our moving, so that the trees, which, one after the other, were rapidly disappearing from my sight, caused me an extreme surprise. "Ah, dear mother!" I exclaimed, "what is this? the trees are walking!" At that very moment the two noblemen came in, and reading astonishment on my countenance, they asked me what my thoughts were so busy about. "How is it," I answered, "that the trees are walking."

They all laughed, but my mother, heaving a great sigh, told me, in a tone of deep pity, "The boat is moving, the trees are not. Now dress yourself."

I understood at once the reason of the phenomenon. "Then it may be," said I, "that the sun does not move, and that we, on the contrary, are revolving from west to east." At these words my good mother fairly screamed. M. Grimani pitied my foolishness, and I remained dismayed, grieved, and ready to cry. M. Baffo brought me life again. He rushed to me, embraced me tenderly, and said, "Thou are right, my child. The sun does not move; take courage, give heed to your reasoning powers and let others laugh."

My mother, greatly surprised, asked him whether he had taken leave of his senses to give me such lessons; but the philosopher, not even condescending to answer her, went on sketching a theory in harmony with my young and simple intelligence. This was the first real pleasure I enjoyed in my life. Had it not been for M. Baffo, this circumstance might have been enough to degrade my understanding; the weakness of credulity would have become part of my mind. The ignorance of the two others would certainly have blunted in me the edge of a faculty which, perhaps, has not carried me very far in my after life, but to which alone I feel that I am indebted for every particle of happiness I enjoy when I look into myself.

We reached Padua at an early hour and went to Ottaviani's house; his wife loaded me with caresses. I found there five or six children, amongst them a girl of eight years, named Marie, and another of seven, Rose, beautiful as a seraph. Ten years later Marie became the wife of the broker Colonda, and Rose, a few years afterwards, married a nobleman, Pierre Marcello, and had one son and two daughters, one of whom was wedded to M. Pierre Moncenigo, and the other to a nobleman of the Carrero family. This last marriage was afterwards nullified. I shall have, in the course of events, to speak of all these persons, and that is my reason for mentioning their names here.

Ottaviani took us at once to the house where I was to board. It was only a few yards from his own residence, at Sainte-Marie d'Advance, in the parish of Saint-Michel, in the house of an old Sclavonian woman, who let the first floor to Signora Mida, wife of a Sclavonian colonel. My small trunk was laid open before the old woman, to whom was handed an inventory of all its contents, together with six sequins for six months paid in advance. For this small sum she undertook to feed me, to keep me clean, and to send me to a day-school. Protesting that it was not enough, she accepted these terms. I was kissed and strongly commanded to be always obedient and docile, and I was left with her.

In this way did my family get rid of me.

CHAPTER II

My Grandmother Comes to Padua, and Takes Me to Dr. Gozzi's School—My
First Love Affair

As soon as I was left alone with the Sclavonian woman, she took me up to the garret, where she pointed out my bed in a row with four others, three of which belonged to three young boys of my age, who at that moment were at school, and the fourth to a servant girl whose province it was to watch us and to prevent the many peccadilloes in which school-boys are wont to indulge. After this visit we came downstairs, and I was taken to the garden with permission to walk about until dinner-time.

I felt neither happy nor unhappy; I had nothing to say. I had neither fear nor hope, nor even a feeling of curiosity; I was neither cheerful nor sad. The only thing which grated upon me was the face of the mistress of the house. Although I had not the faintest idea either of beauty or of ugliness, her face, her countenance, her tone of voice, her language, everything in that woman was repulsive to me. Her masculine features repelled me every time I lifted my eyes towards her face to listen to what she said to me. She was tall and coarse like a trooper; her complexion was yellow, her hair black, her eyebrows long and thick, and her chin gloried in a respectable bristly beard: to complete the picture, her hideous, half-naked bosom was hanging half-way down her long chest; she may have been about fifty. The servant was a stout country girl, who did all the work of the house; the garden was a square of some thirty feet, which had no other beauty than its green appearance.

Towards noon my three companions came back from school, and they at once spoke to me as if we had been old acquaintances, naturally giving me credit for such intelligence as belonged to my age, but which I did not possess. I did not answer them, but they were not baffled, and they at last prevailed upon me to share their innocent pleasures. I had to run, to carry and be carried, to turn head over heels, and I allowed myself to be initiated into those arts with a pretty good grace until we were summoned to dinner. I sat down to the table; but seeing before me a wooden spoon, I pushed it back, asking for my silver spoon and fork to which I was much attached, because they were a gift from my good old granny. The servant answered that the mistress wished to maintain equality between the boys, and I had to submit, much to my disgust. Having thus learned that equality in everything was the rule of the house, I went to work like the others and began to eat the soup out of the common dish, and if I did not complain of the rapidity with which my companions made it disappear, I could not help wondering at such inequality being allowed. To follow this very poor soup, we had a small portion of dried cod and one apple each, and dinner was over: it was in Lent. We had neither glasses nor cups, and we all helped ourselves out of the same earthen pitcher to a miserable drink called graspia, which is made by boiling in water the stems of grapes stripped of their fruit. From the following day I drank nothing but water. This way of living surprised me, for I did not know whether I had a right to complain of it. After dinner the servant took me to the school, kept by a young priest, Doctor Gozzi, with whom the Sclavonian woman had bargained for my schooling at the rate of forty sous a month, or the eleventh part of a sequin.

The first thing to do was to teach me writing, and I was placed amongst children of five and six years, who did not fail to turn me into ridicule on account of my age.

On my return to the boarding-house I had my supper, which, as a matter of course, was worse than the dinner, and I could not make out why the right of complaint should be denied me. I was then put to bed, but there three well-known species of vermin kept me awake all night, besides the rats, which, running all over the garret, jumped on my bed and fairly made my blood run cold with fright. This is the way in which I began to feel misery, and to learn how to suffer it patiently. The vermin, which feasted upon me, lessened my fear of the rats, and by a very lucky system of compensation, the dread of the rats made me less sensitive to the bites of the vermin. My mind was reaping benefit from the very struggle fought between the evils which surrounded me. The servant was perfectly deaf to my screaming.

As soon as it was daylight I ran out of the wretched garret, and, after complaining to the girl of all I had endured during the night, I asked her to give me a clean shirt, the one I had on being disgusting to look at, but she answered that I could only change my linen on a Sunday, and laughed at me when I threatened to complain to the mistress. For the first time in my life I shed tears of sorrow and of anger, when I heard my companions scoffing at me. The poor wretches shared my unhappy condition, but they were used to it, and that makes all the difference.

Sorely depressed, I went to school, but only to sleep soundly through the morning. One of my comrades, in the hope of turning the affair into ridicule at my expense, told the doctor the reason of my being so sleepy. The good priest, however, to whom without doubt Providence had guided me, called me into his private room, listened to all I had to say, saw with his own eyes the proofs of my misery, and moved by the sight of the blisters which disfigured my innocent skin, he took up his cloak, went with me to my boarding-house, and shewed the woman the state I was in. She put on a look of great astonishment, and threw all the blame upon the servant. The doctor being curious to see my bed, I was, as much as he was, surprised at the filthy state of the sheets in which I had passed the night. The accursed woman went on blaming the servant, and said that she would discharge her; but the girl, happening to be close by, and not relishing the accusation, told her boldly that the fault was her own, and she then threw open the beds of my companions to shew us that they did not experience any better treatment. The mistress, raving, slapped her on the face, and the servant, to be even with her, returned the compliment and ran away. The doctor left me there, saying that I could not enter his school unless I was sent to him as clean as the other boys. The result for me was a very sharp rebuke, with the threat, as a finishing stroke, that if I ever caused such a broil again, I would be ignominiously turned out of the house.

I could not make it out; I had just entered life, and I had no knowledge of any other place but the house in which I had been born, in which I had been brought up, and in which I had always seen cleanliness and honest comfort. Here I found myself ill-treated, scolded, although it did not seem possible that any blame could be attached to me. At last the old shrew tossed a shirt in my face, and an hour later I saw a new servant changing the sheets, after which we had our dinner.

My schoolmaster took particular care in instructing me. He gave me a seat at his own desk, and in order to shew my proper appreciation of such a favour, I gave myself up to my studies; at the end of the first month I could write so well that I was promoted to the grammar class.

The new life I was leading, the half-starvation system to which I was condemned, and most likely more than everything else, the air of Padua, brought me health such as I had never enjoyed before, but that very state of blooming health made it still more difficult for me to bear the hunger which I was compelled to endure; it became unbearable. I was growing rapidly; I enjoyed nine hours of deep sleep, unbroken by any dreams, save that I always fancied myself sitting at a well-spread table, and gratifying my cruel appetite, but every morning I could realize in full the vanity and the unpleasant disappointment of flattering dreams! This ravenous appetite would at last have weakened me to death, had I not made up my mind to pounce upon, and to swallow, every kind of eatables I could find, whenever I was certain of not being seen.

Necessity begets ingenuity. I had spied in a cupboard of the kitchen some fifty red herrings; I devoured them all one after the other, as well as all the sausages which were hanging in the chimney to be smoked; and in order to accomplish those feats without being detected, I was in the habit of getting up at night and of undertaking my foraging expeditions under the friendly veil of darkness. Every new-laid egg I could discover in the poultry-yard, quite warm and scarcely dropped by the hen, was a most delicious treat. I would even go as far as the kitchen of the schoolmaster in the hope of pilfering something to eat.

The Sclavonian woman, in despair at being unable to catch the thieves, turned away servant after servant. But, in spite of all my expeditions, as I could not always find something to steal, I was as thin as a walking skeleton.

My progress at school was so rapid during four or five months that the master promoted me to the rank of dux. My province was to examine the lessons of my thirty school-fellows, to correct their mistakes and report to the master with whatever note of blame or of approval I thought they deserved; but my strictness did not last long, for idle boys soon found out the way to enlist my sympathy. When their Latin lesson was full of mistakes, they would buy me off with cutlets and roast chickens; they even gave me money. These proceedings excited my covetousness, or, rather, my gluttony, and, not satisfied with levying a tax upon the ignorant, I became a tyrant, and I refused well-merited approbation to all those who declined paying the contribution I demanded. At last, unable to bear my injustice any longer, the boys accused me, and the master, seeing me convicted of extortion, removed me from my exalted position. I would very likely have fared badly after my dismissal, had not Fate decided to put an end to my cruel apprenticeship.

Doctor Gozzi, who was attached to me, called me privately one day into his study, and asked me whether I would feel disposed to carry out the advice he would give me in order to bring about my removal from the house of the Sclavonian woman, and my admission in his own family. Finding me delighted at such an offer, he caused me to copy three letters which I sent, one to the Abbe Grimani, another to my friend Baffo, and the last to my excellent grandam. The half-year was nearly out, and my mother not being in Venice at that period there was no time to lose.

In my letters I gave a description of all my sufferings, and I prognosticated my death were I not immediately removed from my boarding-house and placed under the care of my school-master, who was disposed to receive me; but he wanted two sequins a month.

M. Grimani did not answer me, and commissioned his friend Ottaviani to scold me for allowing myself to be ensnared by the doctor; but M. Baffo went to consult with my grandmother, who could not write, and in a letter which he addressed to me he informed me that I would soon find myself in a happier situation. And, truly, within a week the excellent old woman, who loved me until her death, made her appearance as I was sitting down to my dinner. She came in with the mistress of the house, and the moment I saw her I threw my arms around her neck, crying bitterly, in which luxury the old lady soon joined me. She sat down and took me on her knees; my courage rose again. In the presence of the Sclavonian woman I enumerated all my grievances, and after calling her attention to the food, fit only for beggars, which I was compelled to swallow, I took her upstairs to shew her my bed. I begged her to take me out and give me a good dinner after six months of such starvation. The boarding-house keeper boldly asserted that she could not afford better for the amount she had received, and there was truth in that, but she had no business to keep house and to become the tormentor of poor children who were thrown on her hands by stinginess, and who required to be properly fed.

My grandmother very quietly intimated her intention to take me away forthwith, and asked her to put all my things in my trunk. I cannot express my joy during these preparations. For the first time I felt that kind of happiness which makes forgiveness compulsory upon the being who enjoys it, and causes him to forget all previous unpleasantness. My grandmother took me to the inn, and dinner was served, but she could hardly eat anything in her astonishment at the voracity with which I was swallowing my food. In the meantime Doctor Gozzi, to whom she had sent notice of her arrival, came in, and his appearance soon prepossessed her in his favour. He was then a fine-looking priest, twenty-six years of age, chubby, modest, and respectful. In less than a quarter of an hour everything was satisfactorily arranged between them. The good old lady counted out twenty-four sequins for one year of my schooling, and took a receipt for the same, but she kept me with her for three days in order to have me clothed like a priest, and to get me a wig, as the filthy state of my hair made it necessary to have it all cut off.

At the end of the three days she took me to the doctor's house, so as to see herself to my installation and to recommend me to the doctor's mother, who desired her to send or to buy in Padua a bedstead and bedding; but the doctor having remarked that, his own bed being very wide, I might sleep with him, my grandmother expressed her gratitude for all his kindness, and we accompanied her as far as the burchiello she had engaged to return to Venice.

The family of Doctor Gozzi was composed of his mother, who had great reverence for him, because, a peasant by birth, she did not think herself worthy of having a son who was a priest, and still more a doctor in divinity; she was plain, old, and cross; and of his father, a shoemaker by trade, working all day long and never addressing a word to anyone, not even during the meals. He only became a sociable being on holidays, on which occasions he would spend his time with his friends in some tavern, coming home at midnight as drunk as a lord and singing verses from Tasso. When in this blissful state the good man could not make up his mind to go to bed, and became violent if anyone attempted to compel him to lie down. Wine alone gave him sense and spirit, for when sober he was incapable of attending to the simplest family matter, and his wife often said that he never would have married her had not his friends taken care to give him a good breakfast before he went to the church.

But Doctor Gozzi had also a sister, called Bettina, who at the age of thirteen was pretty, lively, and a great reader of romances. Her father and mother scolded her constantly because she was too often looking out of the window, and the doctor did the same on account of her love for reading. This girl took at once my fancy without my knowing why, and little by little she kindled in my heart the first spark of a passion which, afterwards became in me the ruling one.

Six months after I had been an inmate in the house, the doctor found himself without scholars; they all went away because I had become the sole object of his affection. He then determined to establish a college, and to receive young boys as boarders; but two years passed before he met with any success. During that period he taught me everything he knew; true, it was not much; yet it was enough to open to me the high road to all sciences. He likewise taught me the violin, an accomplishment which proved very useful to me in a peculiar circumstance, the particulars of which I will give in good time. The excellent doctor, who was in no way a philosopher, made me study the logic of the Peripatetics, and the cosmography of the ancient system of Ptolemy, at which I would laugh, teasing the poor doctor with theorems to which he could find no answer. His habits, moreover, were irreproachable, and in all things connected with religion, although no bigot, he was of the greatest strictness, and, admitting everything as an article of faith, nothing appeared difficult to his conception. He believed the deluge to have been universal, and he thought that, before that great cataclysm, men lived a thousand years and conversed with God, that Noah took one hundred years to build the ark, and that the earth, suspended in the air, is firmly held in the very centre of the universe which God had created from nothing. When I would say and prove that it was absurd to believe in the existence of nothingness, he would stop me short and call me a fool.

He could enjoy a good bed, a glass of wine, and cheerfulness at home. He did not admire fine wits, good jests or criticism, because it easily turns to slander, and he would laugh at the folly of men reading newspapers which, in his opinion, always lied and constantly repeated the same things. He asserted that nothing was more troublesome than incertitude, and therefore he condemned thought because it gives birth to doubt.

His ruling passion was preaching, for which his face and his voice qualified him; his congregation was almost entirely composed of women of whom, however, he was the sworn enemy; so much so, that he would not look them in the face even when he spoke to them. Weakness of the flesh and fornication appeared to him the most monstrous of sins, and he would be very angry if I dared to assert that, in my estimation, they were the most venial of faults. His sermons were crammed with passages from the Greek authors, which he translated into Latin. One day I ventured to remark that those passages ought to be translated into Italian because women did not understand Latin any more than Greek, but he took offence, and I never had afterwards the courage to allude any more to the matter. Moreover he praised me to his friends as a wonder, because I had learned to read Greek alone, without any assistance but a grammar.

During Lent, in the year 1736, my mother, wrote to the doctor; and, as she was on the point of her departure for St. Petersburg, she wished to see me, and requested him to accompany me to Venice for three or four days. This invitation set him thinking, for he had never seen Venice, never frequented good company, and yet he did not wish to appear a novice in anything. We were soon ready to leave Padua, and all the family escorted us to the 'burchiello'.

My mother received the doctor with a most friendly welcome; but she was strikingly beautiful, and my poor master felt very uncomfortable, not daring to look her in the face, and yet called upon to converse with her. She saw the dilemma he was in, and thought she would have some amusing sport about it should opportunity present itself. I, in the meantime, drew the attention of everyone in her circle; everybody had known me as a fool, and was amazed at my improvement in the short space of two years. The doctor was overjoyed, because he saw that the full credit of my transformation was given to him.

The first thing which struck my mother unpleasantly was my light-coloured wig, which was not in harmony with my dark complexion, and contrasted most woefully with my black eyes and eyebrows. She inquired from the doctor why I did not wear my own hair, and he answered that, with a wig, it was easier for his sister to keep me clean. Everyone smiled at the simplicity of the answer, but the merriment increased when, to the question made by my mother whether his sister was married, I took the answer upon myself, and said that Bettina was the prettiest girl of Padua, and was only fourteen years of age. My mother promised the doctor a splendid present for his sister on condition that she would let me wear my own hair, and he promised that her wishes would be complied with. The peruke-maker was then called, and I had a wig which matched my complexion.

Soon afterwards all the guests began to play cards, with the exception of my master, and I went to see my brothers in my grandmother's room. Francois shewed me some architectural designs which I pretended to admire; Jean had nothing to skew me, and I thought him a rather insignificant boy. The others were still very young.

At the supper-table, the doctor, seated next to my mother, was very awkward. He would very likely not have said one word, had not an Englishman, a writer of talent, addressed him in Latin; but the doctor, being unable to make him out, modestly answered that he did not understand English, which caused much hilarity. M. Baffo, however, explained the puzzle by telling us that Englishmen read and pronounced Latin in the same way that they read and spoke their own language, and I remarked that Englishmen were wrong as much as we would be, if we pretended to read and to pronounce their language according to Latin rules. The Englishman, pleased with my reasoning, wrote down the following old couplet, and gave it to me to read:

'Dicite, grammatici, cur mascula nomina cunnus,
Et cur femineum mentula nomen habet.'

After reading it aloud, I exclaimed, "This is Latin indeed."

"We know that," said my mother, "but can you explain it?"

"To explain it is not enough," I answered; "it is a question which is worthy of an answer." And after considering for a moment, I wrote the following pentameter:

'Disce quod a domino nomina servus habet.'

This was my first literary exploit, and I may say that in that very instant the seed of my love for literary fame was sown in my breast, for the applause lavished upon me exalted me to the very pinnacle of happiness. The Englishman, quite amazed at my answer, said that no boy of eleven years had ever accomplished such a feat, embraced me repeatedly, and presented me with his watch. My mother, inquisitive like a woman, asked M. Grimani to tell her the meaning of the lines, but as the abbe was not any wiser than she was M. Baffo translated it in a whisper. Surprised at my knowledge, she rose from her chair to get a valuable gold watch and presented to my master, who, not knowing how to express his deep gratitude, treated us to the most comic scene. My mother, in order to save him from the difficulty of paying her a compliment, offered him her cheek. He had only to give her a couple of kisses, the easiest and the most innocent thing in good company; but the poor man was on burning coals, and so completely out of countenance that he would, I truly believe, rather have died than give the kisses. He drew back with his head down, and he was allowed to remain in peace until we retired for the night.

When we found ourselves alone in our room, he poured out his heart, and exclaimed that it was a pity he could not publish in Padua the distich and my answer.

"And why not?" I said.

"Because both are obscene."

"But they are sublime."

"Let us go to bed and speak no more on the subject. Your answer was wonderful, because you cannot possibly know anything of the subject in question, or of the manner in which verses ought to be written."

As far as the subject was concerned, I knew it by theory; for, unknown to the doctor, and because he had forbidden it, I had read

Meursius, but it was natural that he should be amazed at my being able to write verses, when he, who had taught me prosody, never could compose a single line. 'Nemo dat quod non habet' is a false axiom when applied to mental acquirements.

Four days afterwards, as we were preparing for our departure, my mother gave me a parcel for Bettina, and M. Grimani presented me with four sequins to buy books. A week later my mother left for St. Petersburg.

After our return to Padua, my good master for three or four months never ceased to speak of my mother, and Bettina, having found in the parcel five yards of black silk and twelve pairs of gloves, became singularly attached to me, and took such good care of my hair that in less than six months I was able to give up wearing the wig. She used to comb my hair every morning, often before I was out of bed, saying that she had not time to wait until I was dressed. She washed my face, my neck, my chest; lavished on me childish caresses which I thought innocent, but which caused me to, be angry with myself, because I felt that they excited me. Three years younger than she was, it seemed to me that she could not love me with any idea of mischief, and the consciousness of my own vicious excitement put me out of temper with myself. When, seated on my bed, she would say that I was getting stouter, and would have the proof of it with her own hands, she caused me the most intense emotion; but I said nothing, for fear she would remark my sensitiveness, and when she would go on saying that my skin was soft, the tickling sensation made me draw back, angry with myself that I did not dare to do the same to her, but delighted at her not guessing how I longed to do it. When I was dressed, she often gave me the sweetest kisses, calling me her darling child, but whatever wish I had to follow her example, I was not yet bold enough. After some time, however,

Bettina laughing at my timidity, I became more daring and returned her kisses with interest, but I always gave way the moment I felt a wish to go further; I then would turn my head, pretending to look for something, and she would go away. She was scarcely out of the room before I was in despair at not having followed the inclination of my nature, and, astonished at the fact that Bettina could do to me all she was in the habit of doing without feeling any excitement from it, while I could hardly refrain from pushing my attacks further, I would every day determine to change my way of acting.

In the early part of autumn, the doctor received three new boarders; and one of them, who was fifteen years old, appeared to me in less than a month on very friendly terms with Bettina.

This circumstance caused me a feeling of which until then I had no idea, and which I only analyzed a few years afterwards. It was neither jealousy nor indignation, but a noble contempt which I thought ought not to be repressed, because Cordiani, an ignorant, coarse boy, without talent or polite education, the son of a simple farmer, and incapable of competing with me in anything, having over me but the advantage of dawning manhood, did not appear to me a fit person to be preferred to me; my young self-esteem whispered that I was above him. I began to nurse a feeling of pride mixed with contempt which told against Bettina, whom I loved unknown to myself. She soon guessed it from the way I would receive her caresses, when she came to comb my hair while I was in bed; I would repulse her hands, and no longer return her kisses. One day, vexed at my answering her question as to the reason of my change towards her by stating that I had no cause for it, she, told me in a tone of commiseration that I was jealous of Cordiani. This reproach sounded to me like a debasing slander. I answered that Cordiani was, in my estimation, as worthy of her as she was worthy of him. She went away smiling, but, revolving in her mind the only way by which she could be revenged, she thought herself bound to render me jealous. However, as she could not attain such an end without making me fall in love with her, this is the policy she adopted.

One morning she came to me as I was in bed and brought me a pair of white stockings of her own knitting. After dressing my hair, she asked my permission to try the stockings on herself, in order to correct any deficiency in the other pairs she intended to knit for me. The doctor had gone out to say his mass. As she was putting on the stocking, she remarked that my legs were not clean, and without any more ado she immediately began to wash them. I would have been ashamed to let her see my bashfulness; I let her do as she liked, not foreseeing what would happen. Bettina, seated on my bed, carried too far her love for cleanliness, and her curiosity caused me such intense voluptuousness that the feeling did not stop until it could be carried no further. Having recovered my calm, I bethought myself that I was guilty and begged her forgiveness. She did not expect this, and, after considering for a few moments, she told me kindly that the fault was entirely her own, but that she never would again be guilty of it. And she went out of the room, leaving me to my own thoughts.

They were of a cruel character. It seemed to me that I had brought dishonour upon Bettina, that I had betrayed the confidence of her family, offended against the sacred laws of hospitality, that I was guilty of a most wicked crime, which I could only atone for by marrying her, in case Bettina could make up her mind to accept for her husband a wretch unworthy of her.

These thoughts led to a deep melancholy which went on increasing from day to day, Bettina having entirely ceased her morning visits by my bedside. During the first week, I could easily account for the girl's reserve, and my sadness would soon have taken the character of the warmest love, had not her manner towards Cordiani inoculated in my veins the poison of jealousy, although I never dreamed of accusing her of the same crime towards him that she had committed upon me.

I felt convinced, after due consideration, that the act she had been guilty of with me had been deliberately done, and that her feelings of repentance kept her away from me. This conviction was rather flattering to my vanity, as it gave me the hope of being loved, and the end of all my communings was that I made up my mind to write to her, and thus to give her courage.

I composed a letter, short but calculated to restore peace to her mind, whether she thought herself guilty, or suspected me of feelings contrary to those which her dignity might expect from me. My letter was, in my own estimation, a perfect masterpiece, and just the kind of epistle by which I was certain to conquer her very adoration, and to sink for ever the sun of Cordiani, whom I could not accept as the sort of being likely to make her hesitate for one instant in her choice between him and me. Half-an-hour after the receipt of my letter, she told me herself that the next morning she would pay me her usual visit, but I waited in vain. This conduct provoked me almost to madness, but my surprise was indeed great when, at the breakfast table, she asked me whether I would let her dress me up as a girl to accompany her five or six days later to a ball for which a neighbour of ours, Doctor Olivo, had sent letters of invitation. Everybody having seconded the motion, I gave my consent. I thought this arrangement would afford a favourable opportunity for an explanation, for mutual vindication, and would open a door for the most complete reconciliation, without fear of any surprise arising from the proverbial weakness of the flesh. But a most unexpected circumstance prevented our attending the ball, and brought forth a comedy with a truly tragic turn.

Doctor Gozzi's godfather, a man advanced in age, and in easy circumstances, residing in the country, thought himself, after a severe illness, very near his end, and sent to the doctor a carriage with a request to come to him at once with his father, as he wished them to be present at his death, and to pray for his departing soul. The old shoemaker drained a bottle, donned his Sunday clothes, and went off with his son.

I thought this a favourable opportunity and determined to improve it, considering that the night of the ball was too remote to suit my impatience. I therefore managed to tell Bettina that I would leave ajar the door of my room, and that I would wait for her as soon as everyone in the house had gone to bed. She promised to come. She slept on the ground floor in a small closet divided only by a partition from her father's chamber; the doctor being away, I was alone in the large room. The three boarders had their apartment in a different part of the house, and I had therefore no mishap to fear. I was delighted at the idea that I had at last reached the moment so ardently desired.

The instant I was in my room I bolted my door and opened the one leading to the passage, so that Bettina should have only to push it in order to come in; I then put my light out, but did not undress. When we read of such situations in a romance we think they are exaggerated; they are not so, and the passage in which Ariosto represents Roger waiting for Alcine is a beautiful picture painted from nature.

Until midnight I waited without feeling much anxiety; but I heard the clock strike two, three, four o'clock in the morning without seeing Bettina; my blood began to boil, and I was soon in a state of furious rage. It was snowing hard, but I shook from passion more than from cold. One hour before day-break, unable to master any longer my impatience, I made up my mind to go downstairs with bare feet, so as not to wake the dog, and to place myself at the bottom of the stairs within a yard of Bettina's door, which ought to have been opened if she had gone out of her room. I reached the door; it was closed, and as it could be locked only from inside I imagined that Bettina had fallen asleep. I was on the point of knocking at the door, but was prevented by fear of rousing the dog, as from that door to that of her closet there was a distance of three or four yards. Overwhelmed with grief, and unable to take a decision, I sat down on the last step of the stairs; but at day-break, chilled, benumbed, shivering with cold, afraid that the servant would see me and would think I was mad, I determined to go back to my room. I arise, but at that very moment I hear some noise in Bettina's room. Certain that I am going to see her, and hope lending me new strength, I draw nearer to the door. It opens; but instead of Bettina coming out I see Cordiani, who gives me such a furious kick in the stomach that I am thrown at a distance deep in the snow. Without stopping a single instant Cordiani is off, and locks himself up in the room which he shared with the brothers Feltrini.

I pick myself up quickly with the intention of taking my revenge upon Bettina, whom nothing could have saved from the effects of my rage at that moment. But I find her door locked; I kick vigorously against it, the dog starts a loud barking, and I make a hurried retreat to my room, in which I lock myself up, throwing myself in bed to compose and heal up my mind and body, for I was half dead.

Deceived, humbled, ill-treated, an object of contempt to the happy and triumphant Cordiani, I spent three hours ruminating the darkest schemes of revenge. To poison them both seemed to me but a trifle in that terrible moment of bitter misery. This project gave way to another as extravagant, as cowardly-namely, to go at once to her brother and disclose everything to him. I was twelve years of age, and my mind had not yet acquired sufficient coolness to mature schemes of heroic revenge, which are produced by false feelings of honour; this was only my apprenticeship in such adventures.

I was in that state of mind when suddenly I heard outside of my door the gruff voice of Bettina's mother, who begged me to come down, adding that her daughter was dying. As I would have been very sorry if she had departed this life before she could feel the effects of my revenge, I got up hurriedly and went downstairs. I found Bettina lying in her father's bed writhing with fearful convulsions, and surrounded by the whole family. Half dressed, nearly bent in two, she was throwing her body now to the right, now to the left, striking at random with her feet and with her fists, and extricating herself by violent shaking from the hands of those who endeavoured to keep her down.

With this sight before me, and the night's adventure still in my mind, I hardly knew what to think. I had no knowledge of human nature, no knowledge of artifice and tricks, and I could not understand how I found myself coolly witnessing such a scene, and composedly calm in the presence of two beings, one of whom I intended to kill and the other to dishonour. At the end of an hour Bettina fell asleep.

A nurse and Doctor Olivo came soon after. The first said that the convulsions were caused by hysterics, but the doctor said no, and prescribed rest and cold baths. I said nothing, but I could not refrain from laughing at them, for I knew, or rather guessed, that Bettina's sickness was the result of her nocturnal employment, or of the fright which she must have felt at my meeting with Cordiani. At all events, I determined to postpone my revenge until the return of her brother, although I had not the slightest suspicion that her illness was all sham, for I did not give her credit for so much cleverness.

To return to my room I had to pass through Bettina's closet, and seeing her dress handy on the bed I took it into my head to search her pockets. I found a small note, and recognizing Cordiani's handwriting, I took possession of it to read it in my room. I marvelled at the girl's imprudence, for her mother might have discovered it, and being unable to read would very likely have given it to the doctor, her son. I thought she must have taken leave of her senses, but my feelings may be appreciated when I read the following words: "As your father is away it is not necessary to leave your door ajar as usual. When we leave the supper-table I will go to your closet; you will find me there."

When I recovered from my stupor I gave way to an irresistible fit of laughter, and seeing how completely I had been duped I thought I was cured of my love. Cordiani appeared to me deserving of forgiveness, and Bettina of contempt. I congratulated myself upon having received a lesson of such importance for the remainder of my life. I even went so far as to acknowledge to myself that Bettina had been quite right in giving the preference to Cordiani, who was fifteen years old, while I was only a child. Yet, in spite of my good disposition to forgiveness, the kick administered by Cordiani was still heavy upon my memory, and I could not help keeping a grudge against him.

At noon, as we were at dinner in the kitchen, where we took our meals on account of the cold weather, Bettina began again to raise piercing screams. Everybody rushed to her room, but I quietly kept my seat and finished my dinner, after which I went to my studies. In the evening when I came down to supper I found that Bettina's bed had been brought to the kitchen close by her mother's; but it was no concern of mine, and I remained likewise perfectly indifferent to the noise made during the night, and to the confusion which took place in the morning, when she had a fresh fit of convulsions.

Doctor Gozzi and his father returned in the evening. Cordiani, who felt uneasy, came to inquire from me what my intentions were, but I rushed towards him with an open penknife in my hand, and he beat a hasty retreat. I had entirely abandoned the idea of relating the night's scandalous adventure to the doctor, for such a project I could only entertain in a moment of excitement and rage. The next day the mother came in while we were at our lesson, and told the doctor, after a lengthened preamble, that she had discovered the character of her daughter's illness; that it was caused by a spell thrown over her by a witch, and that she knew the witch well.

"It may be, my dear mother, but we must be careful not to make a mistake.
Who is the witch?"

"Our old servant, and I have just had a proof of it."

"How so?"

"I have barred the door of my room with two broomsticks placed in the shape of a cross, which she must have undone to go in; but when she saw them she drew back, and she went round by the other door. It is evident that, were she not a witch, she would not be afraid of touching them."

"It is not complete evidence, dear mother; send the woman to me."

The servant made her appearance.

"Why," said the doctor, "did you not enter my mother's room this morning through the usual door?"

"I do not know what you mean."

"Did you not see the St. Andrew's cross on the door?"

"What cross is that?"

"It is useless to plead ignorance," said the mother; "where did you sleep last Thursday night?"

"At my niece's, who had just been confined."

"Nothing of the sort. You were at the witches' Sabbath; you are a witch, and have bewitched my daughter."

The poor woman, indignant at such an accusation, spits at her mistress's face; the mistress, enraged, gets hold of a stick to give the servant a drubbing; the doctor endeavours to keep his mother back, but he is compelled to let her loose and to run after the servant, who was hurrying down the stairs, screaming and howling in order to rouse the neighbours; he catches her, and finally succeeds in pacifying her with some money.

After this comical but rather scandalous exhibition, the doctor donned his vestments for the purpose of exorcising his sister and of ascertaining whether she was truly possessed of an unclean spirit. The novelty of this mystery attracted the whole of my attention. All the inmates of the house appeared to me either mad or stupid, for I could not, for the life of me, imagine that diabolical spirits were dwelling in Bettina's body. When we drew near her bed, her breathing had, to all appearance, stopped, and the exorcisms of her brother did not restore it. Doctor Olivo happened to come in at that moment, and inquired whether he would be in the way; he was answered in the negative, provided he had faith.

Upon which he left, saying that he had no faith in any miracles except in those of the Gospel.

Soon after Doctor Gozzi went to his room, and finding myself alone with Bettina I bent down over her bed and whispered in her ear.

"Take courage, get well again, and rely upon my discretion."

She turned her head towards the wall and did not answer me, but the day passed off without any more convulsions. I thought I had cured her, but on the following day the frenzy went up to the brain, and in her delirium she pronounced at random Greek and Latin words without any meaning, and then no doubt whatever was entertained of her being possessed of the evil spirit. Her mother went out and returned soon, accompanied by the most renowned exorcist of Padua, a very ill-featured Capuchin, called Friar Prospero da Bovolenta.

The moment Bettina saw the exorcist, she burst into loud laughter, and addressed to him the most offensive insults, which fairly delighted everybody, as the devil alone could be bold enough to address a Capuchin in such a manner; but the holy man, hearing himself called an obtrusive ignoramus and a stinkard, went on striking Bettina with a heavy crucifix, saying that he was beating the devil. He stopped only when he saw her on the point of hurling at him the chamber utensil which she had just seized. "If it is the devil who has offended thee with his words," she said, "resent the insult with words likewise, jackass that thou art, but if I have offended thee myself, learn, stupid booby, that thou must respect me, and be off at once."

I could see poor Doctor Gozzi blushing; the friar, however, held his ground, and, armed at all points, began to read a terrible exorcism, at the end of which he commanded the devil to state his name.

"My name is Bettina."

"It cannot be, for it is the name of a baptized girl."

"Then thou art of opinion that a devil must rejoice in a masculine name? Learn, ignorant friar, that a devil is a spirit, and does not belong to either sex. But as thou believest that a devil is speaking to thee through my lips, promise to answer me with truth, and I will engage to give way before thy incantations."

"Very well, I agree to this."

"Tell me, then, art thou thinking that thy knowledge is greater than mine?"

"No, but I believe myself more powerful in the name of the holy Trinity, and by my sacred character."

"If thou art more powerful than I, then prevent me from telling thee unpalatable truths. Thou art very vain of thy beard, thou art combing and dressing it ten times a day, and thou would'st not shave half of it to get me out of this body. Cut off thy beard, and I promise to come out."

"Father of lies, I will increase thy punishment a hundred fold."

"I dare thee to do it."

After saying these words, Bettina broke into such a loud peal of laughter, that I could not refrain from joining in it. The Capuchin, turning towards Doctor Gozzi, told him that I was wanting in faith, and that I ought to leave the room; which I did, remarking that he had guessed rightly. I was not yet out of the room when the friar offered his hand to Bettina for her to kiss, and I had the pleasure of seeing her spit upon it.

This strange girl, full of extraordinary talent, made rare sport of the friar, without causing any surprise to anyone, as all her answers were attributed to the devil. I could not conceive what her purpose was in playing such a part.

The Capuchin dined with us, and during the meal he uttered a good deal of nonsense. After dinner, he returned to Bettina's chamber, with the intention of blessing her, but as soon as she caught sight of him, she took up a glass full of some black mixture sent from the apothecary, and threw it at his head. Cordiani, being close by the friar, came in for a good share of the liquid-an accident which afforded me the greatest delight. Bettina was quite right to improve her opportunity, as everything she did was, of course, put to the account of the unfortunate devil. Not overmuch pleased, Friar Prospero, as he left the house, told the doctor that there was no doubt of the girl being possessed, but that another exorcist must be sent for, since he had not, himself, obtained God's grace to eject the evil spirit.

After he had gone, Bettina kept very calm for six hours, and in the evening, to our great surprise, she joined us at the supper table. She told her parents that she felt quite well, spoke to her brother, and then, addressing me, she remarked that, the ball taking place on the morrow, she would come to my room in the morning to dress my hair like a girl's. I thanked her, and said that, as she had been so ill, she ought to nurse herself. She soon retired to bed, and we remained at the table, talking of her.

When I was undressing for the night, I took up my night-cap, and found in it a small note with these words: "You must accompany me to the ball, disguised as a girl, or I will give you a sight which will cause you to weep."

I waited until the doctor was asleep, and I wrote the following answer: "I cannot go to the ball, because I have fully made up my mind to avoid every opportunity of being alone with you. As for the painful sight with which you threaten to entertain me, I believe you capable of keeping your word, but I entreat you to spare my heart, for I love you as if you were my sister. I have forgiven you, dear Bettina, and I wish to forget everything. I enclose a note which you must be delighted to have again in your possession. You see what risk you were running when you left it in your pocket. This restitution must convince you of my friendship."

CHAPTER III

Bettina Is Supposed to Go Mad—Father Mancia—The Small-pox—I Leave
Padua

Bettina must have been in despair, not knowing into whose hands her letter had fallen; to return it to her and thus to allay her anxiety, was therefore a great proof of friendship; but my generosity, at the same time that it freed her from a keen sorrow, must have caused her another quite as dreadful, for she knew that I was master of her secret. Cordiani's letter was perfectly explicit; it gave the strongest evidence that she was in the habit of receiving him every night, and therefore the story she had prepared to deceive me was useless. I felt it was so, and, being disposed to calm her anxiety as far as I could, I went to her bedside in the morning, and I placed in her hands Cordiani's note and my answer to her letter.

The girl's spirit and talent had won my esteem; I could no longer despise her; I saw in her only a poor creature seduced by her natural temperament. She loved man, and was to be pitied only on account of the consequences. Believing that the view I took of the situation was a right one, I had resigned myself like a reasonable being, and not like a disappointed lover. The shame was for her and not for me. I had only one wish, namely, to find out whether the two brothers Feltrini, Cordiani's companions, had likewise shared Bettina's favours.

Bettina put on throughout the day a cheerful and happy look. In the evening she dressed herself for the ball; but suddenly an attack of sickness, whether feigned or real I did not know, compelled her to go to bed, and frightened everybody in the house.

As for myself, knowing the whole affair, I was prepared for new scenes, and indeed for sad ones, for I felt that I had obtained over her a power repugnant to her vanity and self-love. I must, however, confess that, in spite of the excellent school in which I found myself before I had attained manhood, and which ought to have given me experience as a shield for the future, I have through the whole of my life been the dupe of women. Twelve years ago, if it had not been for my guardian angel, I would have foolishly married a young, thoughtless girl, with whom I had fallen in love: Now that I am seventy-two years old I believe myself no longer susceptible of such follies; but, alas! that is the very thing which causes me to be miserable.

The next day the whole family was deeply grieved because the devil of whom Bettina was possessed had made himself master of her reason. Doctor Gozzi told me that there could not be the shadow of a doubt that his unfortunate sister was possessed, as, if she had only been mad, she never would have so cruelly ill-treated the Capuchin, Prospero, and he determined to place her under the care of Father Mancia.

This Mancia was a celebrated Jacobin (or Dominican) exorcist, who enjoyed the reputation of never having failed to cure a girl possessed of the demon.

Sunday had come; Bettina had made a good dinner, but she had been frantic all through the day. Towards midnight her father came home, singing Tasso as usual, and so drunk that he could not stand. He went up to Bettina's bed, and after kissing her affectionately he said to her: "Thou art not mad, my girl."

Her answer was that he was not drunk.

"Thou art possessed of the devil, my dear child."

"Yes, father, and you alone can cure me."

"Well, I am ready."

Upon this our shoemaker begins a theological discourse, expatiating upon the power of faith and upon the virtue of the paternal blessing. He throws off his cloak, takes a crucifix with one hand, places the other over the head of his daughter, and addresses the devil in such an amusing way that even his wife, always a stupid, dull, cross-grained old woman, had to laugh till the tears came down her cheeks. The two performers in the comedy alone were not laughing, and their serious countenance added to the fun of the performance. I marvelled at Bettina (who was always ready to enjoy a good laugh) having sufficient control over herself to remain calm and grave. Doctor Gozzi had also given way to merriment; but begged that the farce should come to an end, for he deemed that his father's eccentricities were as many profanations against the sacredness of exorcism. At last the exorcist, doubtless tired out, went to bed saying that he was certain that the devil would not disturb his daughter during the night.

On the morrow, just as we had finished our breakfast, Father Mancia made his appearance. Doctor Gozzi, followed by the whole family, escorted him to his sister's bedside. As for me, I was entirely taken up by the face of the monk. Here is his portrait. His figure was tall and majestic, his age about thirty; he had light hair and blue eyes; his features were those of Apollo, but without his pride and assuming haughtiness; his complexion, dazzling white, was pale, but that paleness seemed to have been given for the very purpose of showing off the red coral of his lips, through which could be seen, when they opened, two rows of pearls. He was neither thin nor stout, and the habitual sadness of his countenance enhanced its sweetness. His gait was slow, his air timid, an indication of the great modesty of his mind.

When we entered the room Bettina was asleep, or pretended to be so. Father Mancia took a sprinkler and threw over her a few drops of holy water; she opened her eyes, looked at the monk, and closed them immediately; a little while after she opened them again, had a better look at him, laid herself on her back, let her arms droop down gently, and with her head prettily bent on one side she fell into the sweetest of slumbers.

The exorcist, standing by the bed, took out his pocket ritual and the stole which he put round his neck, then a reliquary, which he placed on the bosom of the sleeping girl, and with the air of a saint he begged all of us to fall on our knees and to pray, so that God should let him know whether the patient was possessed or only labouring under a natural disease. He kept us kneeling for half an hour, reading all the time in a low tone of voice. Bettina did not stir.

Tired, I suppose, of the performance, he desired to speak privately with Doctor Gozzi. They passed into the next room, out of which they emerged after a quarter of an hour, brought back by a loud peal of laughter from the mad girl, who, when she saw them, turned her back on them. Father Mancia smiled, dipped the sprinkler over and over in the holy water, gave us all a generous shower, and took his leave.

Doctor Gozzi told us that the exorcist would come again on the morrow, and that he had promised to deliver Bettina within three hours if she were truly possessed of the demon, but that he made no promise if it should turn out to be a case of madness. The mother exclaimed that he would surely deliver her, and she poured out her thanks to God for having allowed her the grace of beholding a saint before her death.

The following day Bettina was in a fine frenzy. She began to utter the most extravagant speeches that a poet could imagine, and did not stop when the charming exorcist came into her room; he seemed to enjoy her foolish talk for a few minutes, after which, having armed himself 'cap-a-pie', he begged us to withdraw. His order was obeyed instantly; we left the chamber, and the door remained open. But what did it matter? Who would have been bold enough to go in?

During three long hours we heard nothing; the stillness was unbroken. At noon the monk called us in. Bettina was there sad and very quiet while the exorcist packed up his things. He took his departure, saying he had very good hopes of the case, and requesting that the doctor would send him news of the patient. Bettina partook of dinner in her bed, got up for supper, and the next day behaved herself rationally; but the following circumstance strengthened my opinion that she had been neither insane nor possessed.

It was two days before the Purification of the Holy Virgin. Doctor Gozzi was in the habit of giving us the sacrament in his own church, but he always sent us for our confession to the church of Saint-Augustin, in which the Jacobins of Padua officiated. At the supper table, he told us to prepare ourselves for the next day, and his mother, addressing us, said: "You ought, all of you, to confess to Father Mancia, so as to obtain absolution from that holy man. I intend to go to him myself." Cordiani and the two Feltrini agreed to the proposal; I remained silent, but as the idea was unpleasant to me, I concealed the feeling, with a full determination to prevent the execution of the project.

I had entire confidence in the secrecy of confession, and I was incapable of making a false one, but knowing that I had a right to choose my confessor, I most certainly never would have been so simple as to confess to Father Mancia what had taken place between me and a girl, because he would have easily guessed that the girl could be no other but Bettina. Besides, I was satisfied that Cordiani would confess everything to the monk, and I was deeply sorry.

Early the next morning, Bettina brought me a band for my neck, and gave me the following letter: "Spurn me, but respect my honour and the shadow of peace to which I aspire. No one from this house must confess to Father Mancia; you alone can prevent the execution of that project, and I need not suggest the way to succeed. It will prove whether you have some friendship for me."

I could not express the pity I felt for the poor girl, as I read that note. In spite of that feeling, this is what I answered: "I can well understand that, notwithstanding the inviolability of confession, your mother's proposal should cause you great anxiety; but I cannot see why, in order to prevent its execution, you should depend upon me rather than upon Cordiani who has expressed his acceptance of it. All I can promise you is that I will not be one of those who may go to Father Mancia; but I have no influence over your lover; you alone can speak to him."

She replied: "I have never addressed a word to Cordiani since the fatal night which has sealed my misery, and I never will speak to him again, even if I could by so doing recover my lost happiness. To you alone I wish to be indebted for my life and for my honour."

This girl appeared to me more wonderful than all the heroines of whom I had read in novels. It seemed to me that she was making sport of me with the most barefaced effrontery. I thought she was trying to fetter me again with her chains; and although I had no inclination for them, I made up my mind to render her the service she claimed at my hands, and which she believed I alone could compass. She felt certain of her success, but in what school had she obtained her experience of the human heart? Was it in reading novels? Most likely the reading of a certain class of novels causes the ruin of a great many young girls, but I am of opinion that from good romances they acquire graceful manners and a knowledge of society.

Having made up my mind to shew her every kindness in my power, I took an opportunity, as we were undressing for the night, of telling Doctor Gozzi that, for conscientious motives, I could not confess to Father Mancia, and yet that I did not wish to be an exception in that matter. He kindly answered that he understood my reasons, and that he would take us all to the church of Saint-Antoine. I kissed his hand in token of my gratitude.

On the following day, everything having gone according to her wishes, I saw Bettina sit down to the table with a face beaming with satisfaction. In the afternoon I had to go to bed in consequence of a wound in my foot; the doctor accompanied his pupils to church; and Bettina being alone, availed herself of the opportunity, came to my room and sat down on my bed. I had expected her visit, and I received it with pleasure, as it heralded an explanation for which I was positively longing.

She began by expressing a hope that I would not be angry with her for seizing the first opportunity she had of some conversation with me.

"No," I answered, "for you thus afford me an occasion of assuring you that, my feelings towards you being those of a friend only, you need not have any fear of my causing you any anxiety or displeasure. Therefore Bettina, you may do whatever suits you; my love is no more. You have at one blow given the death-stroke to the intense passion which was blossoming in my heart. When I reached my room, after the ill-treatment I had experienced at Cordiani's hands, I felt for you nothing but hatred; that feeling soon merged into utter contempt, but that sensation itself was in time, when my mind recovered its balance, changed for a feeling of the deepest indifference, which again has given way when I saw what power there is in your mind. I have now become your friend; I have conceived the greatest esteem for your cleverness. I have been the dupe of it, but no matter; that talent of yours does exist, it is wonderful, divine, I admire it, I love it, and the highest homage I can render to it is, in my estimation, to foster for the possessor of it the purest feelings of friendship. Reciprocate that friendship, be true, sincere, and plain dealing. Give up all nonsense, for you have already obtained from me all I can give you. The very thought of love is repugnant to me; I can bestow my love only where I feel certain of being the only one loved. You are at liberty to lay my foolish delicacy to the account of my youthful age, but I feel so, and I cannot help it. You have written to me that you never speak to Cordiani; if I am the cause of that rupture between you, I regret it, and I think that, in the interest of your honour, you would do well to make it up with him; for the future I must be careful never to give him any grounds for umbrage or suspicion. Recollect also that, if you have tempted him by the same manoeuvres which you have employed towards me, you are doubly wrong, for it may be that, if he truly loves you, you have caused him to be miserable."

"All you have just said to me," answered Bettina, "is grounded upon false impressions and deceptive appearances. I do not love Cordiani, and I never had any love for him; on the contrary, I have felt, and I do feel, for him a hatred which he has richly deserved, and I hope to convince you, in spite of every appearance which seems to convict me. As to the reproach of seduction, I entreat you to spare me such an accusation. On our side, consider that, if you had not yourself thrown temptation in my way, I never would have committed towards you an action of which I have deeply repented, for reasons which you do not know, but which you must learn from me. The fault I have been guilty of is a serious one only because I did not foresee the injury it would do me in the inexperienced mind of the ingrate who dares to reproach me with it."

Bettina was shedding tears: all she had said was not unlikely and rather complimentary to my vanity, but I had seen too much. Besides, I knew the extent of her cleverness, and it was very natural to lend her a wish to deceive me; how could I help thinking that her visit to me was prompted only by her self-love being too deeply wounded to let me enjoy a victory so humiliating to herself? Therefore, unshaken in my preconceived opinion, I told her that I placed implicit confidence in all she had just said respecting the state of her heart previous to the playful nonsense which had been the origin of my love for her, and that I promised never in the future to allude again to my accusation of seduction. "But," I continued, "confess that the fire at that time burning in your bosom was only of short duration, and that the slightest breath of wind had been enough to extinguish it. Your virtue, which went astray for only one instant, and which has so suddenly recovered its mastery over your senses, deserves some praise. You, with all your deep adoring love for me, became all at once blind to my sorrow, whatever care I took to make it clear to your sight. It remains for me to learn how that virtue could be so very dear to you, at the very time that Cordiani took care to wreck it every night."

Bettina eyed me with the air of triumph which perfect confidence in victory gives to a person, and said: "You have just reached the point where I wished you to be. You shall now be made aware of things which I could not explain before, owing to your refusing the appointment which I then gave you for no other purpose than to tell you all the truth. Cordiani declared his love for me a week after he became an inmate in our house; he begged my consent to a marriage, if his father made the demand of my hand as soon as he should have completed his studies. My answer was that I did not know him sufficiently, that I could form no idea on the subject, and I requested him not to allude to it any more. He appeared to have quietly given up the matter, but soon after, I found out that it was not the case; he begged me one day to come to his room now and then to dress his hair; I told him I had no time to spare, and he remarked that you were more fortunate. I laughed at this reproach, as everyone here knew that I had the care of you. It was a fortnight after my refusal to Cordiani, that I unfortunately spent an hour with you in that loving nonsense which has naturally given you ideas until then unknown to your senses. That hour made me very happy: I loved you, and having given way to very natural desires, I revelled in my enjoyment without the slightest remorse of conscience. I was longing to be again with you the next morning, but after supper, misfortune laid for the first time its hand upon me. Cordiani slipped in my hands this note and this letter which I have since hidden in a hole in the wall, with the intention of shewing them to you at the first opportunity."

Saying this, Bettina handed me the note and the letter; the first ran as follows: "Admit me this evening in your closet, the door of which, leading to the yard, can be left ajar, or prepare yourself to make the best of it with the doctor, to whom I intend to deliver, if you should refuse my request, the letter of which I enclose a copy."

The letter contained the statement of a cowardly and enraged informer, and would certainly have caused the most unpleasant results. In that letter Cordiani informed the doctor that his sister spent her mornings with me in criminal connection while he was saying his mass, and he pledged himself to enter into particulars which would leave him no doubt.

"After giving to the case the consideration it required," continued Bettina, "I made up my mind to hear that monster; but my determination being fixed, I put in my pocket my father's stilletto, and holding my door ajar I waited for him there, unwilling to let him come in, as my closet is divided only by a thin partition from the room of my father, whom the slightest noise might have roused up. My first question to Cordiani was in reference to the slander contained in the letter he threatened to deliver to my brother: he answered that it was no slander, for he had been a witness to everything that had taken place in the morning through a hole he had bored in the garret just above your bed, and to which he would apply his eye the moment he knew that I was in your room. He wound up by threatening to discover everything to my brother and to my mother, unless I granted him the same favours I had bestowed upon you. In my just indignation I loaded him with the most bitter insults, I called him a cowardly spy and slanderer, for he could not have seen anything but childish playfulness, and I declared to him that he need not flatter himself that any threat would compel me to give the slightest compliance to his wishes. He then begged and begged my pardon a thousand times, and went on assuring me that I must lay to my rigour the odium of the step he had taken, the only excuse for it being in the fervent love I had kindled in his heart, and which made him miserable. He acknowledged that his letter might be a slander, that he had acted treacherously, and he pledged his honour never to attempt obtaining from me by violence favours which he desired to merit only by the constancy of his love. I then thought myself to some extent compelled to say that I might love him at some future time, and to promise that I would not again come near your bed during the absence of my brother. In this way I dismissed him satisfied, without his daring to beg for so much as a kiss, but with the promise that we might now and then have some conversation in the same place. As soon as he left me I went to bed, deeply grieved that I could no longer see you in the absence of my brother, and that I was unable, for fear of consequences, to let you know the reason of my change. Three weeks passed off in that position, and I cannot express what have been my sufferings, for you, of course, urged me to come, and I was always under the painful necessity of disappointing you. I even feared to find myself alone with you, for I felt certain that I could not have refrained from telling you the cause of the change in my conduct. To crown my misery, add that I found myself compelled, at least once a week, to receive the vile Cordiani outside of my room, and to speak to him, in order to check his impatience with a few words. At last, unable to bear up any longer under such misery, threatened likewise by you, I determined to end my agony. I wished to disclose to you all this intrigue, leaving to you the care of bringing a change for the better, and for that purpose I proposed that you should accompany me to the ball disguised as a girl, although I knew it would enrage Cordiani; but my mind was made up. You know how my scheme fell to the ground. The unexpected departure of my brother with my father suggested to both of you the same idea, and it was before receiving Cordiani's letter that I promised to come to you. Cordiani did not ask for an appointment; he only stated that he would be waiting for me in my closet, and I had no opportunity of telling him that I could not allow him to come, any more than I could find time to let you know that I would be with you only after midnight, as I intended to do, for I reckoned that after an hour's talk I would dismiss the wretch to his room. But my reckoning was wrong; Cordiani had conceived a scheme, and I could not help listening to all he had to say about it. His whining and exaggerated complaints had no end. He upbraided me for refusing to further the plan he had concocted, and which he thought I would accept with rapture if I loved him. The scheme was for me to elope with him during holy week, and to run away to Ferrara, where he had an uncle who would have given us a kind welcome, and would soon have brought his father to forgive him and to insure our happiness for life. The objections I made, his answers, the details to be entered into, the explanations and the ways and means to be examined to obviate the difficulties of the project, took up the whole night. My heart was bleeding as I thought of you; but my conscience is at rest, and I did nothing that could render me unworthy of your esteem. You cannot refuse it to me, unless you believe that the confession I have just made is untrue; but you would be both mistaken and unjust. Had I made up my mind to sacrifice myself and to grant favours which love alone ought to obtain, I might have got rid of the treacherous wretch within one hour, but death seemed preferable to such a dreadful expedient. Could I in any way suppose that you were outside of my door, exposed to the wind and to the snow? Both of us were deserving of pity, but my misery was still greater than yours. All these fearful circumstances were written in the book of fate, to make me lose my reason, which now returns only at intervals, and I am in constant dread of a fresh attack of those awful convulsions. They say I am bewitched, and possessed of the demon; I do not know anything about it, but if it should be true I am the most miserable creature in existence." Bettina ceased speaking, and burst into a violent storm of tears, sobs, and groans. I was deeply moved, although I felt that all she had said might be true, and yet was scarcely worthy of belief:

'Forse era ver, ma non pero credibile
A chi del senso suo fosse signor.'

But she was weeping, and her tears, which at all events were not deceptive, took away from me the faculty of doubt. Yet I put her tears to the account of her wounded self-love; to give way entirely I needed a thorough conviction, and to obtain it evidence was necessary, probability was not enough. I could not admit either Cordiani's moderation or Bettina's patience, or the fact of seven hours employed in innocent conversation. In spite of all these considerations, I felt a sort of pleasure in accepting for ready cash all the counterfeit coins that she had spread out before me.

After drying her tears, Bettina fixed her beautiful eyes upon mine, thinking that she could discern in them evident signs of her victory; but I surprised her much by alluding to one point which, with all her cunning, she had neglected to mention in her defence. Rhetoric makes use of nature's secrets in the same way as painters who try to imitate it: their most beautiful work is false. This young girl, whose mind had not been refined by study, aimed at being considered innocent and artless, and she did her best to succeed, but I had seen too good a specimen of her cleverness.

"Well, my dear Bettina," I said, "your story has affected me; but how do you think I am going to accept your convulsions as natural, and to believe in the demoniac symptoms which came on so seasonably during the exorcisms, although you very properly expressed your doubts on the matter?"

Hearing this, Bettina stared at me, remaining silent for a few minutes, then casting her eyes down she gave way to fresh tears, exclaiming now and then: "Poor me! oh, poor me!" This situation, however, becoming most painful to me, I asked what I could do for her. She answered in a sad tone that if my heart did not suggest to me what to do, she did not herself see what she could demand of me.

"I thought," said she, "that I would reconquer my lost influence over your heart, but, I see it too plainly, you no longer feel an interest in me. Go on treating me harshly; go on taking for mere fictions sufferings which are but too real, which you have caused, and which you will now increase. Some day, but too late, you will be sorry, and your repentance will be bitter indeed."

As she pronounced these words she rose to take her leave; but judging her capable of anything I felt afraid, and I detained her to say that the only way to regain my affection was to remain one month without convulsions and without handsome Father Mancia's presence being required.

"I cannot help being convulsed," she answered, "but what do you mean by applying to the Jacobin that epithet of handsome? Could you suppose—?"

"Not at all, not at all—I suppose nothing; to do so would be necessary for me to be jealous. But I cannot help saying that the preference given by your devils to the exorcism of that handsome monk over the incantations of the ugly Capuchin is likely to give birth to remarks rather detrimental to your honour. Moreover, you are free to do whatever pleases you."

Thereupon she left my room, and a few minutes later everybody came home.

After supper the servant, without any question on my part, informed me that Bettina had gone to bed with violent feverish chills, having previously had her bed carried into the kitchen beside her mother's. This attack of fever might be real, but I had my doubts. I felt certain that she would never make up her mind to be well, for her good health would have supplied me with too strong an argument against her pretended innocence, even in the case of Cordiani; I likewise considered her idea of having her bed placed near her mother's nothing but artful contrivance.

The next day Doctor Olivo found her very feverish, and told her brother that she would most likely be excited and delirious, but that it would be the effect of the fever and not the work of the devil. And truly, Bettina was raving all day, but Dr. Gozzi, placing implicit confidence in the physician, would not listen to his mother, and did not send for the Jacobin friar. The fever increased in violence, and on the fourth day the small-pox broke out. Cordiani and the two brothers Feitrini, who had so far escaped that disease, were immediately sent away, but as I had had it before I remained at home.

The poor girl was so fearfully covered with the loathsome eruption, that on the sixth day her skin could not be seen on any part of her body. Her eyes closed, and her life was despaired of, when it was found that her mouth and throat were obstructed to such a degree that she could swallow nothing but a few drops of honey. She was perfectly motionless; she breathed and that was all. Her mother never left her bedside, and I was thought a saint when I carried my table and my books into the patient's room. The unfortunate girl had become a fearful sight to look upon; her head was dreadfully swollen, the nose could no longer be seen, and much fear was entertained for her eyes, in case her life should be spared. The odour of her perspiration was most offensive, but I persisted in keeping my watch by her.

On the ninth day, the vicar gave her absolution, and after administering extreme unction, he left her, as he said, in the hands of God. In the midst of so much sadness, the conversation of the mother with her son, would, in spite of myself, cause me some amount of merriment. The good woman wanted to know whether the demon who was dwelling in her child could still influence her to perform extravagant follies, and what would become of the demon in the case of her daughter's death, for, as she expressed it, she could not think of his being so stupid as to remain in so loathsome a body. She particularly wanted to ascertain whether the demon had power to carry off the soul of her child. Doctor Gozzi, who was an ubiquitarian, made to all those questions answers which had not even the shadow of good sense, and which of course had no other effect than to increase a hundred-fold the perplexity of his poor mother.

During the tenth and eleventh days, Bettina was so bad that we thought every moment likely to be her last. The disease had reached its worst period; the smell was unbearable; I alone would not leave her, so sorely did I pity her. The heart of man is indeed an unfathomable abyss, for, however incredible it may appear, it was while in that fearful state that Bettina inspired me with the fondness which I showed her after her recovery.

On the thirteenth day the fever abated, but the patient began to experience great irritation, owing to a dreadful itching, which no remedy could have allayed as effectually as these powerful words which I kept constantly pouring into her ear: "Bettina, you are getting better; but if you dare to scratch yourself, you will become such a fright that nobody will ever love you." All the physicians in the universe might be challenged to prescribe a more potent remedy against itching for a girl who, aware that she has been pretty, finds herself exposed to the loss of her beauty through her own fault, if she scratches herself.

At last her fine eyes opened again to the light of heaven; she was moved to her own room, but she had to keep her bed until Easter. She inoculated me with a few pocks, three of which have left upon my face everlasting marks; but in her eyes they gave me credit for great devotedness, for they were a proof of my constant care, and she felt that I indeed deserved her whole love. And she truly loved me, and I returned her love, although I never plucked a flower which fate and prejudice kept in store for a husband. But what a contemptible husband!

Two years later she married a shoemaker, by name Pigozzo—a base, arrant knave who beggared and ill-treated her to such an extent that her brother had to take her home and to provide for her. Fifteen years afterwards, having been appointed arch-priest at Saint-George de la Vallee, he took her there with him, and when I went to pay him a visit eighteen years ago, I found Bettina old, ill, and dying. She breathed her last in my arms in 1776, twenty-four hours after my arrival. I will speak of her death in good time.

About that period, my mother returned from St. Petersburg, where the Empress Anne Iwanowa had not approved of the Italian comedy. The whole of the troop had already returned to Italy, and my mother had travelled with Carlin Bertinazzi, the harlequin, who died in Paris in the year 1783. As soon as she had reached Padua, she informed Doctor Gozzi of her arrival, and he lost no time in accompanying me to the inn where she had put up. We dined with her, and before bidding us adieu, she presented the doctor with a splendid fur, and gave me the skin of a lynx for Bettina. Six months afterwards she summoned me to Venice, as she wished to see me before leaving for Dresden, where she had contracted an engagement for life in the service of the Elector of Saxony, Augustus III., King of Poland. She took with her my brother Jean, then eight years old, who was weeping bitterly when he left; I thought him very foolish, for there was nothing very tragic in that departure. He is the only one in the family who was wholly indebted to our mother for his fortune, although he was not her favourite child.

I spent another year in Padua, studying law in which I took the degree of Doctor in my sixteenth year, the subject of my thesis being in the civil law, 'de testamentis', and in the canon law, 'utrum Hebraei possint construere novas synagogas'.

My vocation was to study medicine, and to practice it, for I felt a great inclination for that profession, but no heed was given to my wishes, and I was compelled to apply myself to the study of the law, for which I had an invincible repugnance. My friends were of opinion that I could not make my fortune in any profession but that of an advocate, and, what is still worse, of an ecclesiastical advocate. If they had given the matter proper consideration, they would have given me leave to follow my own inclinations, and I would have been a physician—a profession in which quackery is of still greater avail than in the legal business. I never became either a physician or an advocate, and I never would apply to a lawyer, when I had any legal business, nor call in a physician when I happened to be ill. Lawsuits and pettifoggery may support a good many families, but a greater proportion is ruined by them, and those who perish in the hands, of physicians are more numerous by far than those who get cured strong evidence in my opinion, that mankind would be much less miserable without either lawyers or doctors.

To attend the lectures of the professors, I had to go to the university called the Bo, and it became necessary for me to go out alone. This was a matter of great wonder to me, for until then I had never considered myself a free man; and in my wish to enjoy fully the liberty I thought I had just conquered, it was not long before I had made the very worst acquaintances amongst the most renowned students. As a matter of course, the most renowned were the most worthless, dissolute fellows, gamblers, frequenters of disorderly houses, hard drinkers, debauchees, tormentors and suborners of honest girls, liars, and wholly incapable of any good or virtuous feeling. In the company of such men did I begin my apprenticeship of the world, learning my lesson from the book of experience.

The theory of morals and its usefulness through the life of man can be compared to the advantage derived by running over the index of a book before reading it when we have perused that index we know nothing but the subject of the work. This is like the school for morals offered by the sermons, the precepts, and the tales which our instructors recite for our especial benefit. We lend our whole attention to those lessons, but when an opportunity offers of profiting by the advice thus bestowed upon us, we feel inclined to ascertain for ourselves whether the result will turn out as predicted; we give way to that very natural inclination, and punishment speedily follows with concomitant repentance. Our only consolation lies in the fact that in such moments we are conscious of our own knowledge, and consider ourselves as having earned the right to instruct others; but those to whom we wish to impart our experience act exactly as we have acted before them, and, as a matter of course, the world remains in statu quo, or grows worse and worse.

When Doctor Gozzi granted me the privilege of going out alone, he gave me an opportunity for the discovery of several truths which, until then, were not only unknown to me, but the very existence of which I had never suspected. On my first appearance, the boldest scholars got hold of me and sounded my depth. Finding that I was a thorough freshman, they undertook my education, and with that worthy purpose in view they allowed me to fall blindly into every trap. They taught me gambling, won the little I possessed, and then they made me play upon trust, and put me up to dishonest practices in order to procure the means of paying my gambling debts; but I acquired at the same time the sad experience of sorrow! Yet these hard lessons proved useful, for they taught me to mistrust the impudent sycophants who openly flatter their dupes, and never to rely upon the offers made by fawning flatterers. They taught me likewise how to behave in the company of quarrelsome duellists, the society of whom ought to be avoided, unless we make up our mind to be constantly in the very teeth of danger. I was not caught in the snares of professional lewd women, because not one of them was in my eyes as pretty as Bettina, but I did not resist so well the desire for that species of vain glory which is the reward of holding life at a cheap price.

In those days the students in Padua enjoyed very great privileges, which were in reality abuses made legal through prescription, the primitive characteristic of privileges, which differ essentially from prerogatives. In fact, in order to maintain the legality of their privileges, the students often committed crimes. The guilty were dealt with tenderly, because the interest of the city demanded that severity should not diminish the great influx of scholars who flocked to that renowned university from every part of Europe. The practice of the Venetian government was to secure at a high salary the most celebrated professors, and to grant the utmost freedom to the young men attending their lessons. The students acknowledged no authority but that of a chief, chosen among themselves, and called syndic. He was usually a foreign nobleman, who could keep a large establishment, and who was responsible to the government for the behaviour of the scholars. It was his duty to give them up to justice when they transgressed the laws, and the students never disputed his sentence, because he always defended them to the utmost, when they had the slightest shadow of right on their side.

The students, amongst other privileges, would not suffer their trunks to be searched by customhouse authorities, and no ordinary policeman would have dared to arrest one of them. They carried about them forbidden weapons, seduced helpless girls, and often disturbed the public peace by their nocturnal broils and impudent practical jokes; in one word, they were a body of young fellows, whom nothing could restrain, who would gratify every whim, and enjoy their sport without regard or consideration for any human being.

It was about that time that a policeman entered a coffee-room, in which were seated two students. One of them ordered him out, but the man taking no notice of it, the student fired a pistol at him, and missed his aim. The policeman returned the fire, wounded the aggressor, and ran away. The students immediately mustered together at the Bo, divided into bands, and went over the city, hunting the policemen to murder them, and avenge the insult they had received. In one of the encounters two of the students were killed, and all the others, assembling in one troop, swore never to lay their arms down as long as there should be one policeman alive in Padua. The authorities had to interfere, and the syndic of the students undertook to put a stop to hostilities provided proper satisfaction was given, as the police were in the wrong. The man who had shot the student in the coffee-room was hanged, and peace was restored; but during the eight days of agitation, as I was anxious not to appear less brave than my comrades who were patrolling the city, I followed them in spite of Doctor Gozzi's remonstrances. Armed with a carbine and a pair of pistols, I ran about the town with the others, in quest of the enemy, and I recollect how disappointed I was because the troop to which I belonged did not meet one policeman. When the war was over, the doctor laughed at me, but Bettina admired my valour. Unfortunately, I indulged in expenses far above my means, owing to my unwillingness to seem poorer than my new friends. I sold or pledged everything I possessed, and I contracted debts which I could not possibly pay. This state of things caused my first sorrows, and they are the most poignant sorrows under which a young man can smart. Not knowing which way to turn, I wrote to my excellent grandmother, begging her assistance, but instead of sending me some money, she came to Padua on the 1st of October, 1739, and, after thanking the doctor and Bettina for all their affectionate care, she bought me back to Venice. As he took leave of me, the doctor, who was shedding tears, gave me what he prized most on earth; a relic of some saint, which perhaps I might have kept to this very day, had not the setting been of gold. It performed only one miracle, that of being of service to me in a moment of great need. Whenever I visited Padua, to complete my study of the law, I stayed at the house of the kind doctor, but I was always grieved at seeing near Bettina the brute to whom she was engaged, and who did not appear to me deserving of such a wife. I have always regretted that a prejudice, of which I soon got rid, should have made me preserve for that man a flower which I could have plucked so easily.

CHAPTER IV

I receive the minor orders from the patriarch of Venice—I get acquainted with Senator Malipiero, with Therese Imer, with the niece of the Curate, with Madame Orio, with Nanette and Marton, and with the Cavamacchia—I become a preacher—my adventure with Lucie at Pasean A rendezvous on the third story.

"He comes from Padua, where he has completed his studies." Such were the words by which I was everywhere introduced, and which, the moment they were uttered, called upon me the silent observation of every young man of my age and condition, the compliments of all fathers, and the caresses of old women, as well as the kisses of a few who, although not old, were not sorry to be considered so for the sake of embracing a young man without impropriety. The curate of Saint-Samuel, the Abbe Josello, presented me to Monsignor Correre, Patriarch of Venice, who gave me the tonsure, and who, four months afterwards, by special favour, admitted me to the four minor orders. No words could express the joy and the pride of my grandmother. Excellent masters were given to me to continue my studies, and M. Baffo chose the Abbe Schiavo to teach me a pure Italian style, especially poetry, for which I had a decided talent. I was very comfortably lodged with my brother Francois, who was studying theatrical architecture. My sister and my youngest brother were living with our grandam in a house of her own, in which it was her wish to die, because her husband had there breathed his last. The house in which I dwelt was the same in which my father had died, and the rent of which my mother continued to pay. It was large and well furnished.

Although Abbe Grimani was my chief protector, I seldom saw him, and I particularly attached myself to M. de Malipiero, to whom I had been presented by the Curate Josello. M. de Malipiero was a senator, who was unwilling at seventy years of age to attend any more to State affairs, and enjoyed a happy, sumptuous life in his mansion, surrounded every evening by a well-chosen party of ladies who had all known how to make the best of their younger days, and of gentlemen who were always acquainted with the news of the town. He was a bachelor and wealthy, but, unfortunately, he had three or four times every year severe attacks of gout, which always left him crippled in some part or other of his body, so that all his person was disabled. His head, his lungs, and his stomach had alone escaped this cruel havoc. He was still a fine man, a great epicure, and a good judge of wine; his wit was keen, his knowledge of the world extensive, his eloquence worthy of a son of Venice, and he had that wisdom which must naturally belong to a senator who for forty years has had the management of public affairs, and to a man who has bid farewell to women after having possessed twenty mistresses, and only when he felt himself compelled to acknowledge that he could no longer be accepted by any woman. Although almost entirely crippled, he did not appear to be so when he was seated, when he talked, or when he was at table. He had only one meal a day, and always took it alone because, being toothless and unable to eat otherwise than very slowly, he did not wish to hurry himself out of compliment to his guests, and would have been sorry to see them waiting for him. This feeling deprived him of the pleasure he would have enjoyed in entertaining at his board friendly and agreeable guests, and caused great sorrow to his excellent cook.

The first time I had the honour of being introduced to him by the curate, I opposed earnestly the reason which made him eat his meals in solitude, and I said that his excellency had only to invite guests whose appetite was good enough to enable them to eat a double share.

"But where can I find such table companions?" he asked.

"It is rather a delicate matter," I answered; "but you must take your guests on trial, and after they have been found such as you wish them to be, the only difficulty will be to keep them as your guests without their being aware of the real cause of your preference, for no respectable man could acknowledge that he enjoys the honour of sitting at your excellency's table only because he eats twice as much as any other man."

The senator understood the truth of my argument, and asked the curate to bring me to dinner on the following day. He found my practice even better than my theory, and I became his daily guest.

This man, who had given up everything in life except his own self, fostered an amorous inclination, in spite of his age and of his gout. He loved a young girl named Therese Imer, the daughter of an actor residing near his mansion, her bedroom window being opposite to his own. This young girl, then in her seventeenth year, was pretty, whimsical, and a regular coquette. She was practising music with a view to entering the theatrical profession, and by showing herself constantly at the window she had intoxicated the old senator, and was playing with him cruelly. She paid him a daily visit, but always escorted by her mother, a former actress, who had retired from the stage in order to work out her salvation, and who, as a matter of course, had made up her mind to combine the interests of heaven with the works of this world. She took her daughter to mass every day and compelled her to go to confession every week; but every afternoon she accompanied her in a visit to the amorous old man, the rage of whom frightened me when she refused him a kiss under the plea that she had performed her devotions in the morning, and that she could not reconcile herself to the idea of offending the God who was still dwelling in her.

What a sight for a young man of fifteen like me, whom the old man admitted as the only and silent witness of these erotic scenes! The miserable mother applauded her daughter's reserve, and went so far as to lecture the elderly lover, who, in his turn, dared not refute her maxims, which savoured either too much or too little of Christianity, and resisted a very strong inclination to hurl at her head any object he had at hand. Anger would then take the place of lewd desires, and after they had retired he would comfort himself by exchanging with me philosophical considerations.

Compelled to answer him, and not knowing well what to say, I ventured one day upon advising a marriage. He struck me with amazement when he answered that she refused to marry him from fear of drawing upon herself the hatred of his relatives.

"Then make her the offer of a large sum of money, or a position."

"She says that she would not, even for a crown, commit a deadly sin."

"In that case, you must either take her by storm, or banish her for ever from your presence."

"I can do neither one nor the other; physical as well as moral strength is deficient in me."

"Kill her, then."

"That will very likely be the case unless I die first."

"Indeed I pity your excellency."

"Do you sometimes visit her?"

"No, for I might fall in love with her, and I would be miserable."

"You are right."

Witnessing many such scenes, and taking part in many similar conversations, I became an especial favourite with the old nobleman. I was invited to his evening assemblies which were, as I have stated before, frequented by superannuated women and witty men. He told me that in this circle I would learn a science of greater import than Gassendi's philosophy, which I was then studying by his advice instead of Aristotle's, which he turned into ridicule. He laid down some precepts for my conduct in those assemblies, explaining the necessity of my observing them, as there would be some wonder at a young man of my age being received at such parties. He ordered me never to open my lips except to answer direct questions, and particularly enjoined me never to pass an opinion on any subject, because at my age I could not be allowed to have any opinions.

I faithfully followed his precepts, and obeyed his orders so well, that in a few days I had gained his esteem, and become the child of the house, as well as the favourite of all the ladies who visited him. In my character of a young and innocent ecclesiastic, they would ask me to accompany them in their visits to the convents where their daughters or their nieces were educated; I was at all hours received at their houses without even being announced; I was scolded if a week elapsed without my calling upon them, and when I went to the apartments reserved for the young ladies, they would run away, but the moment they saw that the intruder was only I, they would return at once, and their confidence was very charming to me.

Before dinner, M. de Malipiero would often inquire from me what advantages were accruing to me from the welcome I received at the hands of the respectable ladies I had become acquainted with at his house, taking care to tell me, before I could have time to answer, that they were all endowed with the greatest virtue, and that I would give everybody a bad opinion of myself, if I ever breathed one word of disparagement to the high reputation they all enjoyed. In this way he would inculcate in me the wise precept of reserve and discretion.

It was at the senator's house that I made the acquaintance of Madame Manzoni, the wife of a notary public, of whom I shall have to speak very often. This worthy lady inspired me with the deepest attachment, and she gave me the wisest advice. Had I followed it, and profited by it, my life would not have been exposed to so many storms; it is true that in that case, my life would not be worth writing.

All these fine acquaintances amongst women who enjoyed the reputation of being high-bred ladies, gave me a very natural desire to shine by my good looks and by the elegance of my dress; but my father confessor, as well as my grandmother, objected very strongly to this feeling of vanity. On one occasion, taking me apart, the curate told me, with honeyed words, that in the profession to which I had devoted myself my thoughts ought to dwell upon the best means of being agreeable to God, and not on pleasing the world by my fine appearance. He condemned my elaborate curls, and the exquisite perfume of my pomatum. He said that the devil had got hold of me by the hair, that I would be excommunicated if I continued to take such care of it, and concluded by quoting for my benefit these words from an oecumenical council: 'clericus qui nutrit coman, anathema sit'. I answered him with the names of several fashionable perfumed abbots, who were not threatened with excommunication, who were not interfered with, although they wore four times as much powder as I did—for I only used a slight sprinkling—who perfumed their hair with a certain amber-scented pomatum which brought women to the very point of fainting, while mine, a jessamine pomade, called forth the compliment of every circle in which I was received. I added that I could not, much to my regret, obey him, and that if I had meant to live in slovenliness, I would have become a Capuchin and not an abbe.

My answer made him so angry that, three or four days afterwards, he contrived to obtain leave from my grandmother to enter my chamber early in the morning, before I was awake, and, approaching my bed on tiptoe with a sharp pair of scissors, he cut off unmercifully all my front hair, from one ear to the other. My brother Francois was in the adjoining room and saw him, but he did not interfere as he was delighted at my misfortune. He wore a wig, and was very jealous of my beautiful head of hair. Francois was envious through the whole of his life; yet he combined this feeling of envy with friendship; I never could understand him; but this vice of his, like my own vices, must by this time have died of old age.

After his great operation, the abbe left my room quietly, but when I woke up shortly afterwards, and realized all the horror of this unheard-of execution, my rage and indignation were indeed wrought to the highest pitch.

What wild schemes of revenge my brain engendered while, with a looking-glass in my hand, I was groaning over the shameful havoc performed by this audacious priest! At the noise I made my grandmother hastened to my room, and amidst my brother's laughter the kind old woman assured me that the priest would never have been allowed to enter my room if she could have foreseen his intention, and she managed to soothe my passion to some extent by confessing that he had over-stepped the limits of his right to administer a reproof.

But I was determined upon revenge, and I went on dressing myself and revolving in my mind the darkest plots. It seemed to me that I was entitled to the most cruel revenge, without having anything to dread from the terrors of the law. The theatres being open at that time I put on a mask to go out, and I, went to the advocate Carrare, with whom I had become acquainted at the senator's house, to inquire from him whether I could bring a suit against the priest. He told me that, but a short time since, a family had been ruined for having sheared the moustache of a Sclavonian—a crime not nearly so atrocious as the shearing of all my front locks, and that I had only to give him my instructions to begin a criminal suit against the abbe, which would make him tremble. I gave my consent, and begged that he would tell M. de Malipiero in the evening the reason for which I could not go to his house, for I did not feel any inclination to show myself anywhere until my hair had grown again.

I went home and partook with my brother of a repast which appeared rather scanty in comparison to the dinners I had with the old senator. The privation of the delicate and plentiful fare to which his excellency had accustomed me was most painful, besides all the enjoyments from which I was excluded through the atrocious conduct of the virulent priest, who was my godfather. I wept from sheer vexation; and my rage was increased by the consciousness that there was in this insult a certain dash of comical fun which threw over me a ridicule more disgraceful in my estimation than the greatest crime.

I went to bed early, and, refreshed by ten hours of profound slumber, I felt in the morning somewhat less angry, but quite as determined to summon the priest before a court. I dressed myself with the intention of calling upon my advocate, when I received the visit of a skilful hair-dresser whom I had seen at Madame Cantarini's house. He told me that he was sent by M. de Malipiero to arrange my hair so that I could go out, as the senator wished me to dine with him on that very day. He examined the damage done to my head, and said, with a smile, that if I would trust to his art, he would undertake to send me out with an appearance of even greater elegance than I could boast of before; and truly, when he had done, I found myself so good-looking that I considered my thirst for revenge entirely satisfied.

Having thus forgotten the injury, I called upon the lawyer to tell him to stay all proceedings, and I hastened to M. de Malipiero's palace, where, as chance would have it, I met the abbe. Notwithstanding all my joy, I could not help casting upon him rather unfriendly looks, but not a word was said about what had taken place. The senator noticed everything, and the priest took his leave, most likely with feelings of mortified repentance, for this time I most verily deserved excommunication by the extreme studied elegance of my curling hair.

When my cruel godfather had left us, I did not dissemble with M. de Malipiero; I candidly told him that I would look out for another church, and that nothing would induce me to remain under a priest who, in his wrath, could go the length of such proceedings. The wise old man agreed with me, and said that I was quite right: it was the best way to make me do ultimately whatever he liked. In the evening everyone in our circle, being well aware of what had happened, complimented me, and assured me that nothing could be handsomer than my new head-dress. I was delighted, and was still more gratified when, after a fortnight had elapsed, I found that M. de Malipiero did not broach the subject of my returning to my godfather's church. My grandmother alone constantly urged me to return. But this calm was the harbinger of a storm. When my mind was thoroughly at rest on that subject, M. de Malipiero threw me into the greatest astonishment by suddenly telling me that an excellent opportunity offered itself for me to reappear in the church and to secure ample satisfaction from the abbe.

"It is my province," added the senator, "as president of the Confraternity of the Holy Sacrament, to choose the preacher who is to deliver the sermon on the fourth Sunday of this month, which happens to be the second Christmas holiday. I mean to appoint you, and I am certain that the abbe will not dare to reject my choice. What say you to such a triumphant reappearance? Does it satisfy you?"

This offer caused me the greatest surprise, for I had never dreamt of becoming a preacher, and I had never been vain enough to suppose that I could write a sermon and deliver it in the church. I told M. de Malipiero that he must surely be enjoying a joke at my expense, but he answered that he had spoken in earnest, and he soon contrived to persuade me and to make me believe that I was born to become the most renowned preacher of our age as soon as I should have grown fat—a quality which I certainly could not boast of, for at that time I was extremely thin. I had not the shadow of a fear as to my voice or to my elocution, and for the matter of composing my sermon I felt myself equal to the production of a masterpiece.

I told M. de Malipiero that I was ready, and anxious to be at home in order to go to work; that, although no theologian, I was acquainted with my subject, and would compose a sermon which would take everyone by surprise on account of its novelty.

On the following day, when I called upon him, he informed me that the abbe had expressed unqualified delight at the choice made by him, and at my readiness in accepting the appointment; but he likewise desired that I should submit my sermon to him as soon as it was written, because the subject belonging to the most sublime theology he could not allow me to enter the pulpit without being satisfied that I would not utter any heresies. I agreed to this demand, and during the week I gave birth to my masterpiece. I have now that first sermon in my possession, and I cannot help saying that, considering my tender years, I think it a very good one.

I could not give an idea of my grandmother's joy; she wept tears of happiness at having a grandson who had become an apostle. She insisted upon my reading my sermon to her, listened to it with her beads in her hands, and pronounced it very beautiful. M. de Malipiero, who had no rosary when I read it to him, was of opinion that it would not prove acceptable to the parson. My text was from Horace: 'Ploravere suis non respondere favorem speratum meritis'; and I deplored the wickedness and ingratitude of men, through which had failed the design adopted by Divine wisdom for the redemption of humankind. But M. de Malipiero was sorry that I had taken my text from any heretical poet, although he was pleased that my sermon was not interlarded with Latin quotations.

I called upon the priest to read my production; but as he was out I had to wait for his return, and during that time I fell in love with his niece, Angela. She was busy upon some tambour work; I sat down close by her, and telling me that she had long desired to make my acquaintance, she begged me to relate the history of the locks of hair sheared by her venerable uncle.

My love for Angela proved fatal to me, because from it sprang two other love affairs which, in their turn, gave birth to a great many others, and caused me finally to renounce the Church as a profession. But let us proceed quietly, and not encroach upon future events.

On his return home the abbe found me with his niece, who was about my age, and he did not appear to be angry. I gave him my sermon: he read it over, and told me that it was a beautiful academical dissertation, but unfit for a sermon from the pulpit, and he added,

"I will give you a sermon written by myself, which I have never delivered; you will commit it to memory, and I promise to let everybody suppose that it is of your own composition."

"I thank you, very reverend father, but I will preach my own sermon, or none at all."

"At all events, you shall not preach such a sermon as this in my church."

"You can talk the matter over with M. de Malipiero. In the meantime I will take my work to the censorship, and to His Eminence the Patriarch, and if it is not accepted I shall have it printed."

"All very well, young man. The patriarch will coincide with me."

In the evening I related my discussion with the parson before all the guests of M. de Malipiero. The reading of my sermon was called for, and it was praised by all. They lauded me for having with proper modesty refrained from quoting the holy fathers of the Church, whom at my age I could not be supposed to have sufficiently studied, and the ladies particularly admired me because there was no Latin in it but the Text from Horace, who, although a great libertine himself, has written very good things. A niece of the patriarch, who was present that evening, promised to prepare her uncle in my favour, as I had expressed my intention to appeal to him; but M. de Malipiero desired me not to take any steps in the matter until I had seen him on the following day, and I submissively bowed to his wishes.

When I called at his mansion the next day he sent for the priest, who soon made his appearance. As he knew well what he had been sent for, he immediately launched out into a very long discourse, which I did not interrupt, but the moment he had concluded his list of objections I told him that there could not be two ways to decide the question; that the patriarch would either approve or disapprove my sermon.

"In the first case," I added, "I can pronounce it in your church, and no responsibility can possibly fall upon your shoulders; in the second, I must, of course, give way."

The abbe was struck by my determination and he said,

"Do not go to the patriarch; I accept your sermon; I only request you to change your text. Horace was a villain."

"Why do you quote Seneca, Tertullian, Origen, and Boethius? They were all heretics, and must, consequently, be considered by you as worse wretches than Horace, who, after all, never had the chance of becoming a Christian!"

However, as I saw it would please M. de Malipiero, I finally consented to accept, as a substitute for mine, a text offered by the abbe, although it did not suit in any way the spirit of my production; and in order to get an opportunity for a visit to his niece, I gave him my manuscript, saying that I would call for it the next day. My vanity prompted me to send a copy to Doctor Gozzi, but the good man caused me much amusement by returning it and writing that I must have gone mad, and that if I were allowed to deliver such a sermon from the pulpit I would bring dishonour upon myself as well as upon the man who had educated me.

I cared but little for his opinion, and on the appointed day I delivered my sermon in the Church of the Holy Sacrament in the presence of the best society of Venice. I received much applause, and every one predicted that I would certainly become the first preacher of our century, as no young ecclesiastic of fifteen had ever been known to preach as well as I had done. It is customary for the faithful to deposit their offerings for the preacher in a purse which is handed to them for that purpose.

The sexton who emptied it of its contents found in it more than fifty sequins, and several billets-doux, to the great scandal of the weaker brethren. An anonymous note amongst them, the writer of which I thought I had guessed, let me into a mistake which I think better not to relate. This rich harvest, in my great penury, caused me to entertain serious thoughts of becoming a preacher, and I confided my intention to the parson, requesting his assistance to carry it into execution. This gave me the privilege of visiting at his house every day, and I improved the opportunity of conversing with Angela, for whom my love was daily increasing. But Angela was virtuous. She did not object to my love, but she wished me to renounce the Church and to marry her. In spite of my infatuation for her, I could not make up my mind to such a step, and I went on seeing her and courting her in the hope that she would alter her decision.

The priest, who had at last confessed his admiration for my first sermon, asked me, some time afterwards, to prepare another for St. Joseph's Day, with an invitation to deliver it on the 19th of March, 1741. I composed it, and the abbe spoke of it with enthusiasm, but fate had decided that I should never preach but once in my life. It is a sad tale, unfortunately for me very true, which some persons are cruel enough to consider very amusing.

Young and rather self-conceited, I fancied that it was not necessary for me to spend much time in committing my sermon to memory. Being the author, I had all the ideas contained in my work classified in my mind, and it did not seem to me within the range of possibilities that I could forget what I had written. Perhaps I might not remember the exact words of a sentence, but I was at liberty to replace them by other expressions as good, and as I never happened to be at a loss, or to be struck dumb, when I spoke in society, it was not likely that such an untoward accident would befall me before an audience amongst whom I did not know anyone who could intimidate me and cause me suddenly to lose the faculty of reason or of speech. I therefore took my pleasure as usual, being satisfied with reading my sermon morning and evening, in order to impress it upon my memory which until then had never betrayed me.

The 19th of March came, and on that eventful day at four o'clock in the afternoon I was to ascend the pulpit; but, believing myself quite secure and thoroughly master of my subject, I had not the moral courage to deny myself the pleasure of dining with Count Mont-Real, who was then residing with me, and who had invited the patrician Barozzi, engaged to be married to his daughter after the Easter holidays.

I was still enjoying myself with my fine company, when the sexton of the church came in to tell me that they were waiting for me in the vestry. With a full stomach and my head rather heated, I took my leave, ran to the church, and entered the pulpit. I went through the exordium with credit to myself, and I took breathing time; but scarcely had I pronounced the first sentences of the narration, before I forgot what I was saying, what I had to say, and in my endeavours to proceed, I fairly wandered from my subject and I lost myself entirely. I was still more discomforted by a half-repressed murmur of the audience, as my deficiency appeared evident. Several persons left the church, others began to smile, I lost all presence of mind and every hope of getting out of the scrape.

I could not say whether I feigned a fainting fit, or whether I truly swooned; all I know is that I fell down on the floor of the pulpit, striking my head against the wall, with an inward prayer for annihilation.

Two of the parish clerks carried me to the vestry, and after a few moments, without addressing a word to anyone, I took my cloak and my hat, and went home to lock myself in my room. I immediately dressed myself in a short coat, after the fashion of travelling priests, I packed a few things in a trunk, obtained some money from my grandmother, and took my departure for Padua, where I intended to pass my third examination. I reached Padua at midnight, and went to Doctor Gozzi's house, but I did not feel the slightest temptation to mention to him my unlucky adventure.

I remained in Padua long enough to prepare myself for the doctor's degree, which I intended to take the following year, and after Easter I returned to Venice, where my misfortune was already forgotten; but preaching was out of the question, and when any attempt was made to induce me to renew my efforts, I manfully kept to my determination never to ascend the pulpit again.

On the eve of Ascension Day M. Manzoni introduced me to a young courtesan, who was at that time in great repute at Venice, and was nick-named Cavamacchia, because her father had been a scourer. This named vexed her a great deal, she wished to be called Preati, which was her family name, but it was all in vain, and the only concession her friends would make was to call her by her Christian name of Juliette. She had been introduced to fashionable notice by the Marquis de Sanvitali, a nobleman from Parma, who had given her one hundred thousand ducats for her favours. Her beauty was then the talk of everybody in Venice, and it was fashionable to call upon her. To converse with her, and especially to be admitted into her circle, was considered a great boon.

As I shall have to mention her several times in the course of my history, my readers will, I trust, allow me to enter into some particulars about her previous life.

Juliette was only fourteen years of age when her father sent her one day to the house of a Venetian nobleman, Marco Muazzo, with a coat which he had cleaned for him. He thought her very beautiful in spite of the dirty rags in which she was dressed, and he called to see her at her father's shop, with a friend of his, the celebrated advocate, Bastien Uccelli, who; struck by the romantic and cheerful nature of Juliette still more than by her beauty and fine figure, gave her an apartment, made her study music, and kept her as his mistress. At the time of the fair, Bastien took her with him to various public places of resort; everywhere she attracted general attention, and secured the admiration of every lover of the sex. She made rapid progress in music, and at the end of six months she felt sufficient confidence in herself to sign an engagement with a theatrical manager who took her to Vienna to give her a 'castrato' part in one of Metastasio's operas.

The advocate had previously ceded her to a wealthy Jew who, after giving her splendid diamonds, left her also.

In Vienna, Juliette appeared on the stage, and her beauty gained for her an admiration which she would never have conquered by her very inferior talent. But the constant crowd of adorers who went to worship the goddess, having sounded her exploits rather too loudly, the august Maria-Theresa objected to this new creed being sanctioned in her capital, and the beautiful actress received an order to quit Vienna forthwith.

Count Spada offered her his protection, and brought her back to Venice, but she soon left for Padua where she had an engagement. In that city she kindled the fire of love in the breast of Marquis Sanvitali, but the marchioness having caught her once in her own box, and Juliette having acted disrespectfully to her, she slapped her face, and the affair having caused a good deal of noise, Juliette gave up the stage altogether. She came back to Venice, where, made conspicuous by her banishment from Vienna, she could not fail to make her fortune. Expulsion from Vienna, for this class of women, had become a title to fashionable favour, and when there was a wish to depreciate a singer or a dancer, it was said of her that she had not been sufficiently prized to be expelled from Vienna.

After her return, her first lover was Steffano Querini de Papozzes, but in the spring of 1740, the Marquis de Sanvitali came to Venice and soon carried her off. It was indeed difficult to resist this delightful marquis! His first present to the fair lady was a sum of one hundred thousand ducats, and, to prevent his being accused of weakness or of lavish prodigality, he loudly proclaimed that the present could scarcely make up for the insult Juliette had received from his wife—an insult, however, which the courtesan never admitted, as she felt that there would be humiliation in such an acknowledgment, and she always professed to admire with gratitude her lover's generosity. She was right; the admission of the blow received would have left a stain upon her charms, and how much more to her taste to allow those charms to be prized at such a high figure!

It was in the year 1741 that M. Manzoni introduced me to this new Phryne as a young ecclesiastic who was beginning to make a reputation. I found her surrounded by seven or eight well-seasoned admirers, who were burning at her feet the incense of their flattery. She was carelessly reclining on a sofa near Querini. I was much struck with her appearance. She eyed me from head to foot, as if I had been exposed for sale, and telling me, with the air of a princess, that she was not sorry to make my acquaintance, she invited me to take a seat. I began then, in my turn, to examine her closely and deliberately, and it was an easy matter, as the room, although small, was lighted with at least twenty wax candles.

Juliette was then in her eighteenth year; the freshness of her complexion was dazzling, but the carnation tint of her cheeks, the vermilion of her lips, and the dark, very narrow curve of her eyebrows, impressed me as being produced by art rather than nature. Her teeth—two rows of magnificent pearls—made one overlook the fact that her mouth was somewhat too large, and whether from habit, or because she could not help it, she seemed to be ever smiling. Her bosom, hid under a light gauze, invited the desires of love; yet I did not surrender to her charms. Her bracelets and the rings which covered her fingers did not prevent me from noticing that her hand was too large and too fleshy, and in spite of her carefully hiding her feet, I judged, by a telltale slipper lying close by her dress, that they were well proportioned to the height of her figure—a proportion which is unpleasant not only to the Chinese and Spaniards, but likewise to every man of refined taste. We want a tall women to have a small foot, and certainly it is not a modern taste, for Holofernes of old was of the same opinion; otherwise he would not have thought Judith so charming: 'et sandalid ejus rapuerunt oculos ejus'. Altogether I found her beautiful, but when I compared her beauty and the price of one hundred thousand ducats paid for it, I marvelled at my remaining so cold, and at my not being tempted to give even one sequin for the privilege of making from nature a study of the charms which her dress concealed from my eyes.

I had scarcely been there a quarter of an hour when the noise made by the oars of a gondola striking the water heralded the prodigal marquis. We all rose from our seats, and M. Querini hastened, somewhat blushing, to quit his place on the sofa. M. de Sanvitali, a man of middle age, who had travelled much, took a seat near Juliette, but not on the sofa, so she was compelled to turn round. It gave me the opportunity of seeing her full front, while I had before only a side view of her face.

After my introduction to Juliette, I paid her four or five visits, and I thought myself justified, by the care I had given to the examination of her beauty, in saying in M. de Malipiero's draw-room, one evening, when my opinion about her was asked, that she could please only a glutton with depraved tastes; that she had neither the fascination of simple nature nor any knowledge of society, that she was deficient in well-bred, easy manners as well as in striking talents and that those were the qualities which a thorough gentleman liked to find in a woman. This opinion met the general approbation of his friends, but M. de Malipiero kindly whispered to me that Juliette would certainly be informed of the portrait I had drawn of her, and that she would become my sworn enemy. He had guessed rightly.

I thought Juliette very singular, for she seldom spoke to me, and whenever she looked at me she made use of an eye-glass, or she contracted her eye-lids, as if she wished to deny me the honour of seeing her eyes, which were beyond all dispute very beautiful. They were blue, wondrously large and full, and tinted with that unfathomable variegated iris which nature only gives to youth, and which generally disappears, after having worked miracles, when the owner reaches the shady side of forty. Frederick the Great preserved it until his death.

Juliette was informed of the portrait I had given of her to M. de Malipiero's friends by the indiscreet pensioner, Xavier Cortantini. One evening I called upon her with M. Manzoni, and she told him that a wonderful judge of beauty had found flaws in hers, but she took good care not to specify them. It was not difficult to make out that she was indirectly firing at me, and I prepared myself for the ostracism which I was expecting, but which, however, she kept in abeyance fully for an hour. At last, our conversation falling upon a concert given a few days before by Imer, the actor, and in which his daughter, Therese, had taken a brilliant part, Juliette turned round to me and inquired what M. de Malipiero did for Therese. I said that he was educating her. "He can well do it," she answered, "for he is a man of talent; but I should like to know what he can do with you?"

"Whatever he can."

"I am told that he thinks you rather stupid."

As a matter of course, she had the laugh on her side, and I, confused, uncomfortable and not knowing what to say, took leave after having cut a very sorry figure, and determined never again to darken her door. The next day at dinner the account of my adventure caused much amusement to the old senator.

Throughout the summer, I carried on a course of Platonic love with my charming Angela at the house of her teacher of embroidery, but her extreme reserve excited me, and my love had almost become a torment to myself. With my ardent nature, I required a mistress like Bettina, who knew how to satisfy my love without wearing it out. I still retained some feelings of purity, and I entertained the deepest veneration for Angela. She was in my eyes the very palladium of Cecrops. Still very innocent, I felt some disinclination towards women, and I was simple enough to be jealous of even their husbands.

Angela would not grant me the slightest favour, yet she was no flirt; but the fire beginning in me parched and withered me. The pathetic entreaties which I poured out of my heart had less effect upon her than upon two young sisters, her companions and friends: had I not concentrated every look of mine upon the heartless girl, I might have discovered that her friends excelled her in beauty and in feeling, but my prejudiced eyes saw no one but

130

Angela. To every outpouring of my love she answered that she was quite ready to become my wife, and that such was to be the limit of my wishes; when she condescended to add that she suffered as much as I did myself, she thought she had bestowed upon me the greatest of favours.

Such was the state of my mind, when, in the first days of autumn, I received a letter from the Countess de Mont-Real with an invitation to spend some time at her beautiful estate at Pasean. She expected many guests, and among them her own daughter, who had married a Venetian nobleman, and who had a great reputation for wit and beauty, although she had but one eye; but it was so beautiful that it made up for the loss of the other. I accepted the invitation, and Pasean offering me a constant round of pleasures, it was easy enough for me to enjoy myself, and to forget for the time the rigours of the cruel Angela.

I was given a pretty room on the ground floor, opening upon the gardens of Pasean, and I enjoyed its comforts without caring to know who my neighbours were.

The morning after my arrival, at the very moment I awoke, my eyes were delighted with the sight of the charming creature who brought me my coffee. She was a very young girl, but as well formed as a young person of seventeen; yet she had scarcely completed her fourteenth year. The snow of her complexion, her hair as dark as the raven's wing, her black eyes beaming with fire and innocence, her dress composed only of a chemise and a short petticoat which exposed a well-turned leg and the prettiest tiny foot, every detail I gathered in one instant presented to my looks the most original and the most perfect beauty I had ever beheld. I looked at her with the greatest pleasure, and her eyes rested upon me as if we had been old acquaintances.

"How did you find your bed?" she asked.

"Very comfortable; I am sure you made it. Pray, who are you?"

"I am Lucie, the daughter of the gate-keeper: I have neither brothers nor sisters, and I am fourteen years old. I am very glad you have no servant with you; I will be your little maid, and I am sure you will be pleased with me."

Delighted at this beginning, I sat up in my bed and she helped me to put on my dressing-gown, saying a hundred things which I did not understand. I began to drink my coffee, quite amazed at her easy freedom, and struck with her beauty, to which it would have been impossible to remain indifferent. She had seated herself on my bed, giving no other apology for that liberty than the most delightful smile.

I was still sipping my coffee, when Lucie's parents came into my room. She did not move from her place on the bed, but she looked at them, appearing very proud of such a seat. The good people kindly scolded her, begged my forgiveness in her favour, and Lucie left the room to attend to her other duties. The moment she had gone her father and mother began to praise their daughter.

"She is," they said, "our only child, our darling pet, the hope of our old age. She loves and obeys us, and fears God; she is as clean as a new pin, and has but one fault."

"What is that?"

"She is too young."

"That is a charming fault which time will mend."

I was not long in ascertaining that they were living specimens of honesty, of truth, of homely virtues, and of real happiness. I was delighted at this discovery, when Lucie returned as gay as a lark, prettily dressed, her hair done in a peculiar way of her own, and with well-fitting shoes. She dropped a simple courtesy before me, gave a couple of hearty kisses to both her parents, and jumped on her father knees. I asked her to come and sit on my bed, but she answered that she could not take such a liberty now that she was dressed, The simplicity, artlessness, and innocence of the answer seemed to me very enchanting, and brought a smile on my lips. I examined her to see whether she was prettier in her new dress or in the morning's negligee, and I decided in favour of the latter. To speak the truth, Lucie was, I thought, superior in everything, not only to Angela, but even to Bettina.

The hair-dresser made his appearance, and the honest family left my   room.
When I was dressed I went to meet the countess and her amiable daughter.
The day passed off very pleasantly, as is generally the case in the country, when you are amongst agreeable people.

In the morning, the moment my eyes were opened,

I rang the bell, and pretty Lucie came in, simple and natural as before, with her easy manners and wonderful remarks. Her candour, her innocence shone brilliantly all over her person. I could not conceive how, with her goodness, her virtue and her intelligence, she could run the risk of exciting me by coming into my room alone, and with so much familiarity. I fancied that she would not attach much importance to certain slight liberties, and would not prove over-scrupulous, and with that idea I made up my mind to shew her that I fully understood her. I felt no remorse of conscience on the score of her parents, who, in my estimation, were as careless as herself; I had no dread of being the first to give the alarm to her innocence, or to enlighten her mind with the gloomy light of malice, but, unwilling either to be the dupe of feeling or to act against it, I resolved to reconnoitre the ground. I extend a daring hand towards her person, and by an involuntary movement she withdraws, blushes, her cheerfulness disappears, and, turning her head aside as if she were in search of something, she waits until her agitation has subsided. The whole affair had not lasted one minute. She came back, abashed at the idea that she had proved herself rather knowing, and at the dread of having perhaps given a wrong interpretation to an action which might have been, on my part, perfectly innocent, or the result of politeness. Her natural laugh soon returned, and, having rapidly read in her mind all I have just described, I lost no time in restoring her confidence, and, judging that I would venture too much by active operations, I resolved to employ the following morning in a friendly chat during which I could make her out better.

In pursuance of that plan, the next morning, as we were talking, I told her that it was cold, but that she would not feel it if she would lie down near me.

"Shall I disturb you?" she said.

"No; but I am thinking that if your mother happened to come in, she would be angry."

"Mother would not think of any harm."

"Come, then. But Lucie, do you know what danger you are exposing yourself to?"

"Certainly I do; but you are good, and, what is more, you are a priest."

"Come; only lock the door."

"No, no, for people might think.... I do not know what." She laid down close by me, and kept on her chatting, although I did not understand a word of what she said, for in that singular position, and unwilling to give way to my ardent desires, I remained as still as a log.

Her confidence in her safety, confidence which was certainly not feigned, worked upon my feelings to such an extent that I would have been ashamed to take any advantage of it. At last she told me that nine o'clock had struck, and that if old Count Antonio found us as we were, he would tease her with his jokes. "When I see that man," she said, "I am afraid and I run away." Saying these words, she rose from the bed and left the room.

I remained motionless for a long while, stupefied, benumbed, and mastered by the agitation of my excited senses as well as by my thoughts. The next morning, as I wished to keep calm, I only let her sit down on my bed, and the conversation I had with her proved without the shadow of a doubt that her parents had every reason to idolize her, and that the easy freedom of her mind as well as of her behaviour with me was entirely owing to her innocence and to her purity. Her artlessness, her vivacity, her eager curiosity, and the bashful blushes which spread over her face whenever her innocent or jesting remarks caused me to laugh, everything, in fact, convinced me that she was an angel destined to become the victim of the first libertine who would undertake to seduce her. I felt sufficient control over my own feelings to resist any attempt against her virtue which my conscience might afterwards reproach me with. The mere thought of taking advantage of her innocence made me shudder, and my self-esteem was a guarantee to her parents, who abandoned her to me on the strength of the good opinion they entertained of me, that Lucie's honour was safe in my hands. I thought I would have despised myself if I had betrayed the trust they reposed in me. I therefore determined to conquer my feelings, and, with perfect confidence in the victory, I made up my mind to wage war against myself, and to be satisfied with her presence as the only reward of my heroic efforts. I was not yet acquainted with the axiom that "as long as the fighting lasts, victory remains uncertain."

As I enjoyed her conversation much, a natural instinct prompted me to tell her that she would afford me great pleasure if she could come earlier in the morning, and even wake me up if I happened to be asleep, adding, in order to give more weight to my request, that the less I slept the better I felt in health. In this manner I contrived to spend three hours instead of two in her society, although this cunning contrivance of mine did not prevent the hours flying, at least in my opinion, as swift as lightning.

Her mother would often come in as we were talking, and when the good woman found her sitting on my bed she would say nothing, only wondering at my kindness. Lucie would then cover her with kisses, and the kind old soul would entreat me to give her child lessons of goodness, and to cultivate her mind; but when she had left us Lucie did not think herself more unrestrained, and whether in or out of her mother's presence, she was always the same without the slightest change.

If the society of this angelic child afforded me the sweetest delight, it also caused me the most cruel suffering. Often, very often, when her face was close to my lips, I felt the most ardent temptation to smother her with kisses, and my blood was at fever heat when she wished that she had been a sister of mine. But I kept sufficient command over myself to avoid the slightest contact, for I was conscious that even one kiss would have been the spark which would have blown up all the edifice of my reserve. Every time she left me I remained astounded at my own victory, but, always eager to win fresh laurels, I longed for the following morning, panting for a renewal of this sweet yet very dangerous contest.

At the end of ten or twelve days, I felt that there was no alternative but to put a stop to this state of things, or to become a monster in my own eyes; and I decided for the moral side of the question all the more easily that nothing insured me success, if I chose the second alternative. The moment I placed her under the obligation to defend herself Lucie would become a heroine, and the door of my room being open, I might have been exposed to shame and to a very useless repentance. This rather frightened me. Yet, to put an end to my torture, I did not know what to decide. I could no longer resist the effect made upon my senses by this beautiful girl, who, at the break of day and scarcely dressed, ran gaily into my room, came to my bed enquiring how I had slept, bent familiarly her head towards me, and, so to speak, dropped her words on my lips. In those dangerous moments I would turn my head aside; but in her innocence she would reproach me for being afraid when she felt herself so safe, and if I answered that I could not possibly fear a child, she would reply that a difference of two years was of no account.

Standing at bay, exhausted, conscious that every instant increased the ardour which was devouring me, I resolved to entreat from herself the discontinuance of her visits, and this resolution appeared to me sublime and infallible; but having postponed its execution until the following morning, I passed a dreadful night, tortured by the image of Lucie, and by the idea that I would see her in the morning for the last time. I fancied that Lucie would not only grant my prayer, but that she would conceive for me the highest esteem. In the morning, it was barely day-light, Lucie beaming, radiant with beauty, a happy smile brightening her pretty mouth, and her splendid hair in the most fascinating disorder, bursts into my room, and rushes with open arms towards my bed; but when she sees my pale, dejected, and unhappy countenance, she stops short, and her beautiful face taking an expression of sadness and anxiety:

"What ails you?" she asks, with deep sympathy.

"I have had no sleep through the night:"

"And why?"

"Because I have made up my mind to impart to you a project which, although fraught with misery to myself, will at least secure me your esteem."

"But if your project is to insure my esteem it ought to make you very cheerful. Only tell me, reverend sir, why, after calling me 'thou' yesterday, you treat me today respectfully, like a lady? What have I done? I will get your coffee, and you must tell me everything after you have drunk it; I long to hear you."

She goes and returns, I drink the coffee, and seeing that my countenance remains grave she tries to enliven me, contrives to make me smile, and claps her hands for joy. After putting everything in order, she closes the door because the wind is high, and in her anxiety not to lose one word of what I have to say, she entreats artlessly a little place near me. I cannot refuse her, for I feel almost lifeless.

I then begin a faithful recital of the fearful state in which her beauty has thrown me, and a vivid picture of all the suffering I have experienced in trying to master my ardent wish to give her some proof of my love; I explain to her that, unable to endure such torture any longer, I see no other safety but in entreating her not to see me any more. The importance of the subject, the truth of my love, my wish to present my expedient in the light of the heroic effort of a deep and virtuous passion, lend me a peculiar eloquence. I endeavour above all to make her realize the fearful consequences which might follow a course different to the one I was proposing, and how miserable we might be.

At the close of my long discourse Lucie, seeing my eyes wet with tears, throws off the bed-clothes to wipe them, without thinking that in so doing she uncovers two globes, the beauty of which might have caused the wreck of the most experienced pilot. After a short silence, the charming child tells me that my tears make her very unhappy, and that she had never supposed that she could cause them.

"All you have just told me," she added, "proves the sincerity of your great love for me, but I cannot imagine why you should be in such dread of a feeling which affords me the most intense pleasure. You wish to banish me from your presence because you stand in fear of your love, but what would you do if you hated me? Am I guilty because I have pleased you? If it is a crime to have won your affection, I can assure you that I did not think I was committing a criminal action, and therefore you cannot conscientiously punish me. Yet I cannot conceal the truth; I am very happy to be loved by you. As for the danger we run, when we love, danger which I can understand, we can set it at defiance, if we choose, and I wonder at my not fearing it, ignorant as I am, while you, a learned man, think it so terrible. I am astonished that love, which is not a disease, should have made you ill, and that it should have exactly the opposite effect upon me. Is it possible that I am mistaken, and that my feeling towards you should not be love? You saw me very cheerful when I came in this morning; it is because I have been dreaming all night, but my dreams did not keep me awake; only several times I woke up to ascertain whether my dream was true, for I thought I was near you; and every time, finding that it was not so, I quickly went to sleep again in the hope of continuing my happy dream, and every time I succeeded. After such a night, was it not natural for me to be cheerful this morning? My dear abbe, if love is a torment for you I am very sorry, but would it be possible for you to live without love? I will do anything you order me to do, but, even if your cure depended upon it, I would not cease to love you, for that would be impossible. Yet if to heal your sufferings it should be necessary for you to love me no more, you must do your utmost to succeed, for I would much rather see you alive without love, than dead for having loved too much. Only try to find some other plan, for the one you have proposed makes me very miserable. Think of it, there may be some other way which will be less painful. Suggest one more practicable, and depend upon Lucie's obedience."

These words, so true, so artless, so innocent, made me realize the immense superiority of nature's eloquence over that of philosophical intellect. For the first time I folded this angelic being in my arms, exclaiming, "Yes, dearest Lucie, yes, thou hast it in thy power to afford the sweetest relief to my devouring pain; abandon to my ardent kisses thy divine lips which have just assured me of thy love."

An hour passed in the most delightful silence, which nothing interrupted except these words murmured now and then by Lucie, "Oh, God! is it true? is it not a dream?" Yet I respected her innocence, and the more readily that she abandoned herself entirely and without the slightest resistance. At last, extricating herself gently from my arms, she said, with some uneasiness, "My heart begins to speak, I must go;" and she instantly rose. Having somewhat rearranged her dress she sat down, and her mother, coming in at that moment, complimented me upon my good looks and my bright countenance, and told Lucie to dress herself to attend mass. Lucie came back an hour later, and expressed her joy and her pride at the wonderful cure she thought she had performed upon me, for the healthy appearance I was then shewing convinced her of my love much better than the pitiful state in which she had found me in the morning. "If your complete happiness," she said, "rests in my power, be happy; there is nothing that I can refuse you."

The moment she left me, still wavering between happiness and fear, I understood that I was standing on the very brink of the abyss, and that nothing but a most extraordinary determination could prevent me from falling headlong into it.

I remained at Pasean until the end of September, and the last eleven nights of my stay were passed in the undisturbed possession of Lucie, who, secure in her mother's profound sleep, came to my room to enjoy in my arms the most delicious hours. The burning ardour of my love was increased by the abstinence to which I condemned myself, although Lucie did everything in her power to make me break through my determination. She could not fully enjoy the sweetness of the forbidden fruit unless I plucked it without reserve, and the effect produced by our constantly lying in each other's arms was too strong for a young girl to resist. She tried everything she could to deceive me, and to make me believe that I had already, and in reality, gathered the whole flower, but Bettina's lessons had been too efficient to allow me to go on a wrong scent, and I reached the end of my stay without yielding entirely to the temptation she so fondly threw in my way. I promised her to return in the spring; our farewell was tender and very sad, and I left her in a state of mind and of body which must have been the cause of her misfortunes, which, twenty years after, I had occasion to reproach myself with in Holland, and which will ever remain upon my conscience.

A few days after my return to Venice, I had fallen back into all my old habits, and resumed my courtship of Angela in the hope that I would obtain from her, at least, as much as Lucie had granted to me. A certain dread which to-day I can no longer trace in my nature, a sort of terror of the consequences which might have a blighting influence upon my future, prevented me from giving myself up to complete enjoyment. I do not know whether I have ever been a truly honest man, but I am fully aware that the feelings I fostered in my youth were by far more upright than those I have, as I lived on, forced myself to accept. A wicked philosophy throws down too many of these barriers which we call prejudices.

The two sisters who were sharing Angela's embroidery lessons were her intimate friends and the confidantes of all her secrets. I made their acquaintance, and found that they disapproved of her extreme reserve towards me. As I usually saw them with Angela and knew their intimacy with her, I would, when I happened to meet them alone, tell them all my sorrows, and, thinking only of my cruel sweetheart, I never was conceited enough to propose that these young girls might fall in love with me; but I often ventured to speak to them with all the blazing inspiration which was burning in me—a liberty I would not have dared to take in the presence of her whom I loved. True love always begets reserve; we fear to be accused of exaggeration if we should give utterance to feelings inspired, by passion, and the modest lover, in his dread of saying too much, very often says too little.

The teacher of embroidery, an old bigot, who at first appeared not to mind the attachment I skewed for Angela, got tired at last of my too frequent visits, and mentioned them to the abbe, the uncle of my fair lady. He told me kindly one day that I ought not to call at that house so often, as my constant visits might be wrongly construed, and prove detrimental to the reputation of his niece. His words fell upon me like a thunder-bolt, but I mastered my feelings sufficiently to leave him without incurring any suspicion, and I promised to follow his good advice.

Three or four days afterwards, I paid a visit to the teacher of embroidery, and, to make her believe that my visit was only intended for her, I did not stop one instant near the young girls; yet I contrived to slip in the hand of the eldest of the two sisters a note enclosing another for my dear Angela, in which I explained why I had been compelled to discontinue my visits, entreating her to devise some means by which I could enjoy the happiness of seeing her and of conversing with her. In my note to Nanette, I only begged her to give my letter to her friend, adding that I would see them again the day after the morrow, and that I trusted to her to find an opportunity for delivering me the answer. She managed it all very cleverly, and, when I renewed my visit two days afterwards, she gave me a letter without attracting the attention of anyone. Nanette's letter enclosed a very short note from Angela, who, disliking letter-writing, merely advised me to follow, if I could, the plan proposed by her friend. Here is the copy of the letter written by Nanette, which I have always kept, as well as all other letters which I give in these Memoirs:

"There is nothing in the world, reverend sir, that I would not readily do for my friend. She visits at our house every holiday, has supper with us, and sleeps under our roof. I will suggest the best way for you to make the acquaintance of Madame Orio, our aunt; but, if you obtain an introduction to her, you must be very careful not to let her suspect your preference for Angela, for our aunt would certainly object to her house being made a place of rendezvous to facilitate your interviews with a stranger to her family. Now for the plan I propose, and in the execution of which I will give you every assistance in my power. Madame Orio, although a woman of good station in life, is not wealthy, and she wishes to have her name entered on the list of noble widows who receive the bounties bestowed by the Confraternity of the Holy Sacrament, of which M. de Malipiero is president. Last Sunday, Angela mentioned that you are in the good graces of that nobleman, and that the best way to obtain his patronage would be to ask you to entreat it in her behalf. The foolish girl added that you were smitten with me, that all your visits to our mistress of embroidery were made for my special benefit and for the sake of entertaining me, and that I would find it a very easy task to interest you in her favour. My aunt answered that, as you are a priest, there was no fear of any harm, and she told me to write to you with an invitation to call on her; I refused. The procurator Rosa, who is a great favourite of my aunt's, was present; he approved of my refusal, saying that the letter ought to be written by her and not by me, that it was for my aunt to beg the honour of your visit on business of real importance, and that, if there was any truth in the report of your love for me, you would not fail to come. My aunt, by his advice, has therefore written the letter which you will find at your house. If you wish to meet Angela, postpone your visit to us until next Sunday. Should you succeed in obtaining M. de Malipiero's good will in favour of my aunt, you will become the pet of the household, but you must forgive me if I appear to treat you with coolness, for I have said that I do not like you. I would advise you to make love to my aunt, who is sixty years of age; M. Rosa will not be jealous, and you will become dear to everyone. For my part, I will manage for you an opportunity for some private conversation with Angela, and I will do anything to convince you of my friendship. Adieu."

This plan appeared to me very well conceived, and, having the same evening received Madame Orio's letter, I called upon her on the following day, Sunday. I was welcomed in a very friendly manner, and the lady, entreating me to exert in her behalf my influence with M. de Malipiero, entrusted me with all the papers which I might require to succeed. I undertook to do my utmost, and I took care to address only a few words to Angela, but I directed all my gallant attentions to Nanette, who treated me as coolly as could be. Finally, I won the friendship of the old procurator Rosa, who, in after years, was of some service to me.

I had so much at stake in the success of Madame Orio's petition, that I thought of nothing else, and knowing all the power of the beautiful Therese Imer over our amorous senator, who would be but too happy to please her in anything, I determined to call upon her the next day, and I went straight to her room without being announced. I found her alone with the physician Doro, who, feigning to be on a professional visit, wrote a prescription, felt her pulse, and went off. This Doro was suspected of being in love with Therese; M. de Malipiero, who was jealous, had forbidden Therese to receive his visits, and she had promised to obey him. She knew that I was acquainted with those circumstances, and my presence was evidently unpleasant to her, for she had certainly no wish that the old man should hear how she kept her promise. I thought that no better opportunity could be found of obtaining from her everything I wished.

I told her in a few words the object of my visit, and I took care to add that she could rely upon my discretion, and that I would not for the world do her any injury. Therese, grateful for this assurance, answered that she rejoiced at finding an occasion to oblige me, and, asking me to give her the papers of my protege, she shewed me the certificates and testimonials of another lady in favour of whom she had undertaken to speak, and whom, she said, she would sacrifice to the person in whose behalf I felt interested. She kept her word, for the very next day she placed in my hands the brevet, signed by his excellency as president of the confraternity. For the present, and with the expectation of further favours, Madame Orio's name was put down to share the bounties which were distributed twice a year.

Nanette and her sister Marton were the orphan daughters of a sister of Madame Orio. All the fortune of the good lady consisted in the house which was her dwelling, the first floor being let, and in a pension given to her by her brother, member of the council of ten. She lived alone with her two charming nieces, the eldest sixteen, and the youngest fifteen years of age. She kept no servant, and only employed an old woman, who, for one crown a month, fetched water, and did the rough work. Her only friend was the procurator Rosa; he had, like her, reached his sixtieth year, and expected to marry her as soon as he should become a widower.

The two sisters slept together on the third floor in a large bed, which was likewise shared by Angela every Sunday.

As soon as I found myself in possession of the deed for Madame Orio, I hastened to pay a visit to the mistress of embroidery, in order to find an opportunity of acquainting Nanette with my success, and in a short note which I prepared, I informed her that in two days I would call to give the brevet to Madame Orio, and I begged her earnestly not to forget her promise to contrive a private interview with my dear Angela.

When I arrived, on the appointed day, at Madame Orio's house, Nanette, who had watched for my coming, dexterously conveyed to my hand a billet, requesting me to find a moment to read it before leaving the house. I found Madame Orio, Angela, the old procurator, and Marton in the room. Longing to read the note, I refused the seat offered to me, and presenting to Madame Orio the deed she had so long desired, I asked, as my only reward, the pleasure of kissing her hand, giving her to understand that I wanted to leave the room immediately.

"Oh, my dear abbe!" said the lady, "you shall have a kiss, but not on my hand, and no one can object to it, as I am thirty years older than you."

She might have said forty-five without going much astray. I gave her two kisses, which evidently satisfied her, for she desired me to perform the same ceremony with her nieces, but they both ran away, and Angela alone stood the brunt of my hardihood. After this the widow asked me to sit down.

"I cannot, Madame."

"Why, I beg?"

"I have—."

"I understand. Nanette, shew the way."

"Dear aunt, excuse me."

"Well, then, Marton."

"Oh! dear aunt, why do you not insist upon my sister obeying your orders?"

"Alas! madame, these young ladies are quite right. Allow me to retire."

"No, my dear abbe, my nieces are very foolish; M. Rosa, I am sure, will kindly."

The good procurator takes me affectionately by the hand, and leads me to the third story, where he leaves me. The moment I am alone I open my letter, and I read the following:

"My aunt will invite you to supper; do not accept. Go away as soon as we sit down to table, and Marton will escort you as far as the street door, but do not leave the house. When the street door is closed again, everyone thinking you are gone, go upstairs in the dark as far as the third floor, where you must wait for us. We will come up the moment M. Rosa has left the house, and our aunt has gone to bed. Angela will be at liberty to grant you throughout the night a tete-a-tete which, I trust, will prove a happy one."

Oh! what joy-what gratitude for the lucky chance which allowed me to read this letter on the very spot where I was to expect the dear abject of my love! Certain of finding my way without the slightest difficulty, I returned to Madame Orio's sitting-room, overwhelmed with happiness.

CHAPTER V

An Unlucky Night I Fall in Love with the Two Sisters, and Forget
Angela—A Ball at My House—Juliette's Humiliation—My Return   to
Pasian—Lucie's Misfortune—A Propitious Storm

On my reappearance, Madame Orio told me, with many heart-felt thanks, that I must for the future consider myself as a privileged and welcome friend, and the evening passed off very pleasantly. As the hour for supper drew near, I excused myself so well that Madame Orio could not insist upon my accepting her invitation to stay. Marton rose to light me out of the room, but her aunt, believing Nanette to be my favourite, gave her such an imperative order to accompany me that she was compelled to obey. She went down the stairs rapidly, opened and closed the street door very noisily, and putting her light out, she reentered the sitting room, leaving me in darkness. I went upstairs softly: when I reached the third landing I found the chamber of the two sisters, and, throwing myself upon a sofa, I waited patiently for the rising of the star of my happiness. An hour passed amidst the sweetest dreams of my imagination; at last I hear the noise of the street door opening and closing, and, a few minutes after, the two sisters come in with my Angela. I draw her towards me, and caring for nobody else, I keep up for two full hours my conversation with her. The clock strikes midnight; I am pitied for having gone so late supperless, but I am shocked at such an idea; I answer that, with such happiness as I am enjoying, I can suffer from no human want. I am told that I am a prisoner, that the key of the house door is under the aunt's pillow, and that it is opened only by herself as she goes in the morning to the first mass. I wonder at my young friends imagining that such news can be anything but delightful to me. I express all my joy at the certainty of passing the next five hours with the beloved mistress of my heart. Another hour is spent, when suddenly Nanette begins to laugh, Angela wants to know the reason, and Marton whispering a few words to her, they both laugh likewise. This puzzles me. In my turn, I want to know what causes this general laughter, and at last Nanette, putting on an air of anxiety, tells me that they have no more candle, and that in a few minutes we shall be in the dark. This is a piece of news particularly agreeable to me, but I do not let my satisfaction appear on my countenance, and saying how truly I am sorry for their sake, I propose that they should go to bed and sleep quietly under my respectful guardianship. My proposal increases their merriment.

"What can we do in the dark?"

"We can talk."

We were four; for the last three hours we had been talking, and I was the hero of the romance. Love is a great poet, its resources are inexhaustible, but if the end it has in view is not obtained, it feels weary and remains silent. My Angela listened willingly, but little disposed to talk herself, she seldom answered, and she displayed good sense rather than wit. To weaken the force of my arguments, she was often satisfied with hurling at me a proverb, somewhat in the fashion of the Romans throwing the catapult. Every time that my poor hands came to the assistance of love, she drew herself back or repulsed me. Yet, in spite of all, I went on talking and using my hands without losing courage, but I gave myself up to despair when I found that my rather artful arguing astounded her without bringing conviction to her heart, which was only disquieted, never softened. On the other hand, I could see with astonishment upon their countenances the impression made upon the two sisters by the ardent speeches I poured out to Angela. This metaphysical curve struck me as unnatural, it ought to have been an angle; I was then, unhappily for myself, studying geometry. I was in such a state that, notwithstanding the cold, I was perspiring profusely. At last the light was nearly out, and Nanette took it away.

The moment we were in the dark, I very naturally extended my arms to seize her whom I loved; but I only met with empty space, and I could not help laughing at the rapidity with which Angela had availed herself of the opportunity of escaping me. For one full hour I poured out all the tender, cheerful words that love inspired me with, to persuade her to come back to me; I could only suppose that it was a joke to tease me. But I became impatient.

"The joke," I said, "has lasted long enough; it is foolish, as I could not run after you, and I am surprised to hear you laugh, for your strange conduct leads me to suppose that you are making fun of me. Come and take your seat near me, and if I must speak to you without seeing you let my hands assure me that I am not addressing my words to the empty air. To continue this game would be an insult to me, and my love does not deserve such a return."

"Well, be calm. I will listen to every word you may say, but you must feel that it would not be decent for me to place myself near you in this dark room."

"Do you want me to stand where I am until morning?"

"Lie down on the bed, and go to sleep."

"In wonder, indeed, at your thinking me capable of doing so in the state
I am in. Well, I suppose we must play at blind man's buff."

Thereupon, I began to feel right and left, everywhere, but in vain. Whenever I caught anyone it always turned out to be Nanette or Marton, who at once discovered themselves, and I, stupid Don Quixote, instantly would let them go! Love and prejudice blinded me, I could not see how ridiculous I was with my respectful reserve. I had not yet read the anecdotes of Louis XIII, king of France, but I had read Boccacio. I kept on seeking in vain, reproaching her with her cruelty, and entreating her to let me catch her; but she would only answer that the difficulty of meeting each other was mutual. The room was not large, and I was enraged at my want of success.

Tired and still more vexed, I sat down, and for the next hour I told the history of Roger, when Angelica disappears through the power of the magic ring which the loving knight had so imprudently given her:

'Così dicendo, intorno a la fortuna
Brancolando n'andava come cieco.
O quante volte abbraccio l'aria vana
Speyando la donzella abbracciar seco'.

Angela had not read Ariosto, but Nanette had done so several times. She undertook the defence of Angelica, and blamed the simplicity of Roger, who, if he had been wise, would never have trusted the ring to a coquette. I was delighted with Nanette, but I was yet too much of a novice to apply her remarks to myself.

Only one more hour remained, and I was to leave before the break of day, for Madame Orio would have died rather than give way to the temptation of missing the early mass. During that hour I spoke to Angela, trying to convince her that she ought to come and sit by me. My soul went through every gradation of hope and despair, and the reader cannot possibly realize it unless he has been placed in a similar position. I exhausted the most convincing arguments; then I had recourse to prayers, and even to tears; but, seeing all was useless, I gave way to that feeling of noble indignation which lends dignity to anger. Had I not been in the dark, I might, I truly believe, have struck the proud monster, the cruel girl, who had thus for five hours condemned me to the most distressing suffering. I poured out all the abuse, all the insulting words that despised love can suggest to an infuriated mind; I loaded her with the deepest curses; I swore that my love had entirely turned into hatred, and, as a finale, I advised her to be careful, as I would kill her the moment I would set my eyes on her.

My invectives came to an end with the darkness. At the first break of day, and as soon as I heard the noise made by the bolt and the key of the street door, which Madame Orio was opening to let herself out, that she might seek in the church the repose of which her pious soul was in need, I got myself ready and looked for my cloak and for my hat. But how can I ever portray the consternation in which I was thrown when, casting a sly glance upon the young friends, I found the three bathed in tears! In my shame and despair I thought of committing suicide, and sitting down again, I recollected my brutal speeches, and upbraided myself for having wantonly caused them to weep. I could not say one word; I felt choking; at last tears came to my assistance, and I gave way to a fit of crying which relieved me. Nanette then remarked that her aunt would soon return home; I dried my eyes, and, not venturing another look at Angela or at her friends, I ran away without uttering a word, and threw myself on my bed, where sleep would not visit my troubled mind.

At noon, M. de Malipiero, noticing the change in my countenance, enquired what ailed me, and longing to unburden my heart, I told him all that had happened. The wise old man did not laugh at my sorrow, but by his sensible advice he managed to console me and to give me courage. He was in the same predicament with the beautiful Therese. Yet he could not help giving way to his merriment when at dinner he saw me, in spite of my grief, eat with increased appetite; I had gone without my supper the night before; he complimented me upon my happy constitution.

I was determined never to visit Madame Orio's house, and on that very day I held an argument in metaphysics, in which I contended that any being of whom we had only an abstract idea, could only exist abstractedly, and I was right; but it was a very easy task to give to my thesis an irreligious turn, and I was obliged to recant. A few days afterwards I went to Padua, where I took my degree of doctor 'utroque jure'.

When I returned to Venice, I received a note from M. Rosa, who entreated me to call upon Madame Orio; she wished to see me, and, feeling certain of not meeting Angela, I paid her a visit the same evening. The two graceful sisters were so kind, so pleasant, that they scattered to the winds the shame I felt at seeing them after the fearful night I had passed in their room two months before. The labours of writing my thesis and passing my examination were of course sufficient excuses for Madame Orio, who only wanted to reproach me for having remained so long away from her house.

As I left, Nanette gave me a letter containing a note from Angela, the contents of which ran as follows:

"If you are not afraid of passing another night with me you shall have no reason to complain of me, for I love you, and I wish to hear from your own lips whether you would still have loved me if I had consented to become contemptible in your eyes."

This is the letter of Nanette, who alone had her wits about her:

"M. Rosa having undertaken to bring you back to our house, I prepare these few lines to let you know that Angela is in despair at having lost you. I confess that the night you spent with us was a cruel one, but I do not think that you did rightly in giving up your visits to Madame Orio. If you still feel any love for Angela, I advise you to take your chances once more. Accept a rendezvous for another night; she may vindicate herself, and you will be happy. Believe me; come. Farewell!"

Those two letters afforded me much gratification, for I had it in my power to enjoy my revenge by shewing to Angela the coldest contempt. Therefore, on the following Sunday I went to Madame Orio's house, having provided myself with a smoked tongue and a couple of bottles of Cyprus wine; but to my great surprise my cruel mistress was not there. Nanette told me that she had met her at church in the morning, and that she would not be able to come before supper-time. Trusting to that promise I declined Madam Orio's invitation, and before the family sat down to supper I left the room as I had done on the former occasion, and slipped upstairs. I longed to represent the character I had prepared myself for, and feeling assured that Angela, even if she should prove less cruel, would only grant me insignificant favours, I despised them in anticipation, and resolved to be avenged.

After waiting three quarters of an hour the street door was locked, and a moment later Nanette and Marton entered the room.

"Where is Angela?" I enquired.

"She must have been unable to come, or to send a message. Yet she knows you are here."

"She thinks she has made a fool of me; but I suspected she would act in this way. You know her now. She is trifling with me, and very likely she is now revelling in her triumph. She has made use of you to allure me in the snare, and it is all the better for her; had she come, I meant to have had my turn, and to have laughed at her."

"Ah! you must allow me to have my doubts as to that."

"Doubt me not, beautiful Nanette; the pleasant night we are going to spend without her must convince you."

"That is to say that, as a man of sense, you can accept us as a makeshift; but you can sleep here, and my sister can lie with me on the sofa in the next room."

"I cannot hinder you, but it would be great unkindness on your part. At all events, I do not intend to go to bed."

"What! you would have the courage to spend seven hours alone with us? Why, I am certain that in a short time you will be at a loss what to say, and you will fall asleep."

"Well, we shall see. In the mean-time here are provisions. You will not be so cruel as to let me eat alone? Can you get any bread?"

"Yes, and to please you we must have a second supper."

"I ought to be in love with you. Tell me, beautiful Nanette, if I were as much attached to you as I was to Angela, would you follow her example and make me unhappy?"

"How can you ask such a question? It is worthy of a conceited man. All I can answer is, that I do not know what I would do."

They laid the cloth, brought some bread, some Parmesan cheese and water, laughing all the while, and then we went to work. The wine, to which they were not accustomed, went to their heads, and their gaiety was soon delightful. I wondered, as I looked at them, at my having been blind enough not to see their merit.

After our supper, which was delicious, I sat between them, holding their hands, which I pressed to my lips, asking them whether they were truly my friends, and whether they approved of Angela's conduct towards me. They both answered that it had made them shed many tears. "Then let me," I said, "have for you the tender feelings of a brother, and share those feelings yourselves as if you were my sisters; let us exchange, in all innocence, proofs of our mutual affection, and swear to each other an eternal fidelity."

The first kiss I gave them was prompted by entirely harmless motives, and they returned the kiss, as they assured me a few days afterwards only to prove to me that they reciprocated my brotherly feelings; but those innocent kisses, as we repeated them, very soon became ardent ones, and kindled a flame which certainly took us by surprise, for we stopped, as by common consent, after a short time, looking at each other very much astonished and rather serious. They both left me without affection, and I remained alone with my thoughts. Indeed, it was natural that the burning kisses I had given and received should have sent through me the fire of passion, and that I should suddenly have fallen madly in love with the two amiable sisters. Both were handsomer than Angela, and they were superior to her— Nanette by her charming wit, Marton by her sweet and simple nature; I could not understand how I had been so long in rendering them the justice they deserved, but they were the innocent daughters of a noble family, and the lucky chance which had thrown them in my way ought not to prove a calamity for them. I was not vain enough to suppose that they loved me, but I could well enough admit that my kisses had influenced them in the same manner that their kisses had influenced me, and, believing this to be the case, it was evident that, with a little cunning on my part, and of sly practices of which they were ignorant, I could easily, during the long night I was going to spend with them, obtain favours, the consequences of which might be very positive. The very thought made me shudder, and I firmly resolved to respect their virtue, never dreaming that circumstances might prove too strong for me.

When they returned, I read upon their countenances perfect security and satisfaction, and I quickly put on the same appearance, with a full determination not to expose myself again to the danger of their kisses.

For one hour we spoke of Angela, and I expressed my determination never to see her again, as I had every proof that she did not care for me. "She loves you," said the artless Marton; "I know she does, but if you do not mean to marry her, you will do well to give up all intercourse with her, for she is quite determined not to grant you even a kiss as long as you are not her acknowledged suitor. You must therefore either give up the acquaintance altogether, or make up your mind that she will refuse you everything."

"You argue very well, but how do you know that she loves me?"

"I am quite sure of it, and as you have promised to be our brother, I can tell you why I have that conviction. When Angela is in bed with me, she embraces me lovingly and calls me her dear abbe."

The words were scarcely spoken when Nanette, laughing heartily, placed her hand on her sister's lips, but the innocent confession had such an effect upon me that I could hardly control myself.

Marton told Nanette that I could not possibly be ignorant of what takes place between young girls sleeping together.

"There is no doubt," I said, "that everybody knows those trifles, and I do not think, dear Nanette, that you ought to reproach your sister with indiscretion for her friendly confidence."

"It cannot be helped now, but such things ought not to be mentioned.   If Angela knew it!"

"She would be vexed, of course; but Marton has given me a mark of her friendship which I never can forget. But it is all over; I hate Angela, and I do not mean to speak to her any more! she is false, and she wishes my ruin."

"Yet, loving you, is she wrong to think of having you for her husband?"

"Granted that she is not; but she thinks only of her own self, for she knows what I suffer, and her conduct would be very different if she loved me. In the mean time, thanks to her imagination, she finds the means of satisfying her senses with the charming Marton who kindly performs the part of her husband."

159

Nanette laughed louder, but I kept very serious, and I went on talking to her sister, and praising her sincerity. I said that very likely, and to reciprocate her kindness, Angela must likewise have been her husband, but she answered, with a smile, that Angela played husband only to Nanette, and Nanette could not deny it.

"But," said I, "what name did Nanette, in her rapture, give to her husband?"

"Nobody knows."

"Do you love anyone, Nanette?"

"I do; but my secret is my own."

This reserve gave me the suspicion that I had something to do with her secret, and that Nanette was the rival of Angela. Such a delightful conversation caused me to lose the wish of passing an idle night with two girls so well made for love.

"It is very lucky," I exclaimed, "that I have for you only feelings of friendship; otherwise it would be very hard to pass the night without giving way to the temptation of bestowing upon you proofs of my affection, for you are both so lovely, so bewitching, that you would turn the brains of any man."

As I went on talking, I pretended to be somewhat sleepy; Nanette being the first to notice it, said, "Go to bed without any ceremony, we will lie down on the sofa in the adjoining room."

"I would be a very poor-spirited fellow indeed, if I agreed to this; let us talk; my sleepiness will soon pass off, but I am anxious about you. Go to bed yourselves, my charming friends, and I will go into the next room. If you are afraid of me, lock the door, but you would do me an injustice, for I feel only a brother's yearnings towards you."

"We cannot accept such an arrangement," said Nanette, "but let me persuade you; take this bed."

"I cannot sleep with my clothes on."

"Undress yourself; we will not look at you."

"I have no fear of it, but how could I find the heart to sleep, while on my account you are compelled to sit up?"

"Well," said Marton, "we can lie down, too, without undressing."

"If you shew me such distrust, you will offend me. Tell me, Nanette, do you think I am an honest man?"

"Most certainly."

"Well, then, give me a proof of your good opinion; lie down near me in the bed, undressed, and rely on my word of honour that I will not even lay a finger upon you. Besides, you are two against one, what can you fear? Will you not be free to get out of the bed in case I should not keep quiet? In short, unless you consent to give me this mark of your confidence in me, at least when I have fallen asleep, I cannot go to bed."

I said no more, and pretended to be very sleepy. They exchanged a few words, whispering to each other, and Marton told me to go to bed, that they would follow me as soon as I was asleep. Nanette made me the same promise, I turned my back to them, undressed myself quickly, and wishing them good night, I went to bed. I immediately pretended to fall asleep, but soon I dozed in good earnest, and only woke when they came to bed. Then, turning round as if I wished to resume my slumbers, I remained very quiet until I could suppose them fast asleep; at all events, if they did not sleep, they were at liberty to pretend to do so. Their backs were towards me, and the light was out; therefore I could only act at random, and I paid my first compliments to the one who was lying on my right, not knowing whether she was Nanette or Marton. I find her bent in two, and wrapped up in the only garment she had kept on. Taking my time, and sparing her modesty, I compel her by degrees to acknowledge her defeat, and convince her that it is better to feign sleep and to let me proceed. Her natural instincts soon working in concert with mine, I reach the goal; and my efforts, crowned with the most complete success, leave me not the shadow of a doubt that I have gathered those first-fruits to which our prejudice makes us attach so great an importance. Enraptured at having enjoyed my manhood completely and for the first time, I quietly leave my beauty in order to do homage to the other sister. I find her motionless, lying on her back like a person wrapped in profound and undisturbed slumber. Carefully managing my advance, as if I were afraid of waking her up, I begin by gently gratifying her senses, and I ascertain the delightful fact that, like her sister, she is still in possession of her maidenhood. As soon as a natural movement proves to me that love accepts the offering, I take my measures to consummate the sacrifice. At that moment, giving way suddenly to the violence of her feelings, and tired of her assumed dissimulation, she warmly locks me in her arms at the very instant of the voluptuous crisis, smothers me with kisses, shares my raptures, and love blends our souls in the most ecstatic enjoyment.

Guessing her to be Nanette, I whisper her name.

"Yes, I am Nanette," she answers; "and I declare myself happy, as well as my sister, if you prove yourself true and faithful."

"Until death, my beloved ones, and as everything we have done is the work of love, do not let us ever mention the name of Angela."

After this, I begged that she would give us a light; but Marton, always kind and obliging, got out of bed leaving us alone. When I saw Nanette in my arms, beaming with love, and Marton near the bed, holding a candle, with her eyes reproaching us with ingratitude because we did not speak to her, who, by accepting my first caresses, had encouraged her sister to follow her example, I realized all my happiness.

"Let us get up, my darlings," said I, "and swear to each other eternal affection."

When we had risen we performed, all three together, ablutions which made them laugh a good deal, and which gave a new impetus to the ardour of our feelings. Sitting up in the simple costume of nature, we ate the remains of our supper, exchanging those thousand trifling words which love alone can understand, and we again retired to our bed, where we spent a most delightful night giving each other mutual and oft-repeated proofs of our passionate ardour. Nanette was the recipient of my last bounties, for Madame Orio having left the house to go to church, I had to hasten my departure, after assuring the two lovely sisters that they had effectually extinguished whatever flame might still have flickered in my heart for Angela. I went home and slept soundly until dinner-time.

M. de Malipiero passed a remark upon my cheerful looks and the dark circles around my eyes, but I kept my own counsel, and I allowed him to think whatever he pleased. On the following day I paid a visit to Madame Orio, and Angela not being of the party, I remained to supper and retired with M. Rosa. During the evening Nanette contrived to give me a letter and a small parcel. The parcel contained a small lump of wax with the stamp of a key, and the letter told me to have a key made, and to use it to enter the house whenever I wished to spend the night with them. She informed me at the same time that Angela had slept with them the night following our adventures, and that, thanks to their mutual and usual practices, she had guessed the real state of things, that they had not denied it, adding that it was all her fault, and that Angela, after abusing them most vehemently, had sworn never again to darken their doors; but they did not care a jot.

A few days afterwards our good fortune delivered us from Angela; she was taken to Vicenza by her father, who had removed there for a couple of years, having been engaged to paint frescoes in some houses in that city. Thanks to her absence, I found myself undisturbed possessor of the two charming sisters, with whom I spent at least two nights every week, finding no difficulty in entering the house with the key which I had speedily procured.

Carnival was nearly over, when M. Manzoni informed me one day that the celebrated Juliette wished to see me, and regretted much that I had ceased to visit her. I felt curious as to what she had to say to me, and accompanied him to her house. She received me very politely, and remarking that she had heard of a large hall I had in my house, she said she would like to give a ball there, if I would give her the use of it. I readily consented, and she handed me twenty-four sequins for the supper and for the band, undertaking to send people to place chandeliers in the hall and in my other rooms.

M. de Sanvitali had left Venice, and the Parmesan government had placed his estates in chancery in consequence of his extravagant expenditure. I met him at Versailles ten years afterwards. He wore the insignia of the king's order of knighthood, and was grand equerry to the eldest daughter of Louis XV., Duchess of Parma, who, like all the French princesses, could not be reconciled to the climate of Italy.

The ball took place, and went off splendidly. All the guests belonged to Juliette's set, with the exception of Madame Orio, her nieces, and the procurator Rosa, who sat together in the room adjoining the hall, and whom I had been permitted to introduce as persons of no consequence whatever.

While the after-supper minuets were being danced Juliette took me apart, and said, "Take me to your bedroom; I have just got an amusing idea."

My room was on the third story; I shewed her the way. The moment we entered she bolted the door, much to my surprise. "I wish you," she said, "to dress me up in your ecclesiastical clothes, and I will disguise you as a woman with my own things. We will go down and dance together. Come, let us first dress our hair."

Feeling sure of something pleasant to come, and delighted with such an unusual adventure, I lose no time in arranging her hair, and I let her afterwards dress mine. She applies rouge and a few beauty spots to my face; I humour her in everything, and to prove her satisfaction, she gives me with the best of grace a very loving kiss, on condition that I do not ask for anything else.

"As you please, beautiful Juliette, but I give you due notice that I adore you!"

I place upon my bed a shirt, an abbe's neckband, a pair of drawers, black silk stockings—in fact, a complete fit-out. Coming near the bed, Juliette drops her skirt, and cleverly gets into the drawers, which were not a bad fit, but when she comes to the breeches there is some difficulty; the waistband is too narrow, and the only remedy is to rip it behind or to cut it, if necessary. I undertake to make everything right, and, as I sit on the foot of my bed, she places herself in front of me, with her back towards me. I begin my work, but she thinks that I want to see too much, that I am not skilful enough, and that my fingers wander in unnecessary places; she gets fidgety, leaves me, tears the breeches, and manages in her own way. Then I help her to put her shoes on, and I pass the shirt over her head, but as I am disposing the ruffle and the neck-band, she complains of my hands being too curious; and in truth, her bosom was rather scanty. She calls me a knave and rascal, but I take no notice of her. I was not going to be duped, and I thought that a woman who had been paid one hundred thousand ducats was well worth some study. At last, her toilet being completed, my turn comes. In spite of her objections I quickly get rid of my breeches, and she must put on me the chemise, then a skirt, in a word she has to dress me up. But all at once, playing the coquette, she gets angry because I do not conceal from her looks the very apparent proof that her charms have some effect on a particular part of my being, and she refuses to grant me the favour which would soon afford both relief and calm. I try to kiss her, and she repulses me, whereupon I lose patience, and in spite of herself she has to witness the last stage of my excitement. At the sight of this, she pours out every insulting word she can think of; I endeavour to prove that she is to blame, but it is all in vain.

However, she is compelled to complete my disguise. There is no doubt that an honest woman would not have exposed herself to such an adventure, unless she had intended to prove her tender feelings, and that she would not have drawn back at the very moment she saw them shared by her companion; but women like Juliette are often guided by a spirit of contradiction which causes them to act against their own interests. Besides, she felt disappointed when she found out that I was not timid, and my want of restraint appeared to her a want of respect. She would not have objected to my stealing a few light favours which she would have allowed me to take, as being of no importance, but, by doing that, I should have flattered her vanity too highly.

Our disguise being complete, we went together to the dancing-hall, where the enthusiastic applause of the guests soon restored our good temper. Everybody gave me credit for a piece of fortune which I had not enjoyed, but I was not ill-pleased with the rumour, and went on dancing with the false abbe, who was only too charming. Juliette treated me so well during the night that I construed her manners towards me into some sort of repentance, and I almost regretted what had taken place between us; it was a momentary weakness for which I was sorely punished.

At the end of the quadrille all the men thought they had a right to take liberties with the abbe, and I became myself rather free with the young girls, who would have been afraid of exposing themselves to ridicule had they offered any opposition to my caresses.

M. Querini was foolish enough to enquire from me whether I had kept on my breeches, and as I answered that I had been compelled to lend them to Juliette, he looked very unhappy, sat down in a corner of the room, and refused to dance.

Every one of the guests soon remarked that I had on a woman's chemise, and nobody entertained a doubt of the sacrifice having been consummated, with the exception of Nanette and Marton, who could not imagine the possibility of my being unfaithful to them. Juliette perceived that she had been guilty of great imprudence, but it was too late to remedy the evil.

When we returned to my chamber upstairs, thinking that she had repented of her previous behaviour, and feeling some desire to possess her, I thought I would kiss her, and I took hold of her hand, saying I was disposed to give her every satisfaction, but she quickly slapped my face in so violent a manner that, in my indignation, I was very near returning the compliment. I undressed myself rapidly without looking at her, she did the same, and we came downstairs; but, in spite of the cold water I had applied to my cheek, everyone could easily see the stamp of the large hand which had come in contact with my face.

Before leaving the house, Juliette took me apart, and told me, in the most decided and impressive manner, that if I had any fancy for being thrown out of the window, I could enjoy that pleasure whenever I liked to enter her dwelling, and that she would have me murdered if this night's adventure ever became publicly known. I took care not to give her any cause for the execution of either of her threats, but I could not prevent the fact of our having exchanged shirts being rather notorious. As I was not seen at her house, it was generally supposed that she had been compelled by M. Querini to keep me at a distance. The reader will see how, six years later, this extraordinary woman thought proper to feign entire forgetfulness of this adventure.

I passed Lent, partly in the company of my loved ones, partly in the study of experimental physics at the Convent of the

Salutation. My evenings were always given to M. de Malipiero's assemblies. At Easter, in order to keep the promise I had made to the Countess of Mont-Real, and longing to see again my beautiful Lucie, I went to Pasean. I found the guests entirely different to the set I had met the previous autumn. Count Daniel, the eldest of the family, had married a Countess Gozzi, and a young and wealthy government official, who had married a god-daughter of the old countess, was there with his wife and his sister-in-law. I thought the supper very long. The same room had been given to me, and I was burning to see Lucie, whom I did not intend to treat any more like a child. I did not see her before going to bed, but I expected her early the next morning, when lo! instead of her pretty face brightening my eyes, I see standing before me a fat, ugly servant-girl! I enquire after the gatekeeper's family, but her answer is given in the peculiar dialect of the place, and is, of course, unintelligible to me.

I wonder what has become of Lucie; I fancy that our intimacy has been found out, I fancy that she is ill—dead, perhaps. I dress myself with the intention of looking for her. If she has been forbidden to see me, I think to myself, I will be even with them all, for somehow or other I will contrive the means of speaking to her, and out of spite I will do with her that which honour prevented love from accomplishing. As I was revolving such thoughts, the gate-keeper comes in with a sorrowful countenance. I enquire after his wife's health, and after his daughter, but at the name of Lucie his eyes are filled with tears.

"What! is she dead?"

"Would to God she were!"

"What has she done?"

"She has run away with Count Daniel's courier, and we have been unable to trace her anywhere."

His wife comes in at the moment he replies, and at these words, which renewed her grief, the poor woman faints away. The keeper, seeing how sincerely I felt for his misery, tells me that this great misfortune befell them only a week before my arrival.

"I know that man l'Aigle," I say; "he is a scoundrel. Did he ask to marry
Lucie?"

"No; he knew well enough that our consent would have been refused!"

"I wonder at Lucie acting in such a way."

"He seduced her, and her running away made us suspect the truth, for she had become very stout."

"Had he known her long?"

"About a month after your last visit she saw him for the first time. He must have thrown a spell over her, for our Lucie was as pure as a dove, and you can, I believe, bear testimony to her goodness."

"And no one knows where they are?"

"No one. God alone knows what this villain will do with her."

I grieved as much as the unfortunate parents; I went out and took a long ramble in the woods to give way to my sad feelings. During two hours I cogitated over considerations, some true, some false, which were all prefaced by an if. If I had paid this visit, as I might have done, a week sooner, loving Lucie would have confided in me, and I would have prevented that self-murder. If I had acted with her as with Nanette and Marton, she would not have been left by me in that state of ardent excitement which must have proved the principal cause of her fault, and she would not have fallen a prey to that scoundrel. If she had not known me before meeting the courier, her innocent soul would never have listened to such a man. I was in despair, for in my conscience I acknowledged myself the primary agent of this infamous seduction; I had prepared the way for the villain.

Had I known where to find Lucie, I would certainly have gone forth on the instant to seek for her, but no trace whatever of her whereabouts had been discovered.

Before I had been made acquainted with Lucie's misfortune I felt great pride at having had sufficient power over myself to respect her innocence; but after hearing what had happened I was ashamed of my own reserve, and I promised myself that for the future I would on that score act more wisely. I felt truly miserable when my imagination painted the probability of the unfortunate girl being left to poverty and shame, cursing the remembrance of me, and hating me as the first cause of her misery. This fatal event caused me to adopt a new system, which in after years I carried sometimes rather too far.

I joined the cheerful guests of the countess in the gardens, and received such a welcome that I was soon again in my usual spirits, and at dinner I delighted everyone.

My sorrow was so great that it was necessary either to drive it away at once or to leave Pasean. But a new life crept into my being as I examined the face and the disposition of the newly-married lady. Her sister was prettier, but I was beginning to feel afraid of a novice; I thought the work too great.

This newly-married lady, who was between nineteen and twenty years of age, drew upon herself everybody's attention by her over-strained and unnatural manners. A great talker, with a memory crammed with maxims and precepts often without sense, but of which she loved to make a show, very devout, and so jealous of her husband that she did not conceal her vexation when he expressed his satisfaction at being seated at table opposite her sister, she laid herself open to much ridicule. Her husband was a giddy young fellow, who perhaps felt very deep affection for his wife, but who imagined that, through good breeding, he ought to appear very indifferent, and whose vanity found pleasure in giving her constant causes for jealousy. She, in her turn, had a great dread of passing for an idiot if she did not shew her appreciation of, and her resentment for, his conduct. She felt uneasy in the midst of good company, precisely because she wished to appear thoroughly at home. If I prattled away with some of my trilling nonsense, she would stare at me, and in her anxiety not to be thought stupid, she would laugh out of season. Her oddity, her awkwardness, and her self-conceit gave me the desire to know her better, and I began to dance attendance upon her.

My attentions, important and unimportant, my constant care, ever my fopperies, let everybody know that I meditated conquest. The husband was duly warned, but, with a great show of intrepidity, he answered with a joke every time he was told that I was a formidable rival. On my side I assumed a modest, and even sometimes a careless appearance, when, to shew his freedom from jealousy, he excited me to make love to his wife, who, on her part, understood but little how to perform the part of fancy free.

I had been paying my address to her for five or six days with great constancy, when, taking a walk with her in the garden, she imprudently confided to me the reason of her anxiety respecting her husband, and how wrong he was to give her any cause for jealousy. I told her, speaking as an old friend, that the best way to punish him would be to take no apparent notice of her, husband's preference for her sister, and to feign to be herself in love with me. In order to entice her more easily to follow my advice, I added that I was well aware of my plan being a very difficult one to carry out, and that to play successfully such a character a woman must be particularly witty. I had touched her weak point, and she exclaimed that she would play the part to perfection; but in spite of her self-confidence she acquitted herself so badly that everybody understood that the plan was of my own scheming.

If I happened to be alone with her in the dark paths of the garden, and tried to make her play her part in real earnest, she would take the dangerous step of running away, and rejoining the other guests; the result being that, on my reappearance, I was called a bad sportsman who frightened the bird away. I would not fail at the first opportunity to reproach her for her flight, and to represent the triumph she had thus prepared for her spouse. I praised her mind, but lamented over the shortcomings of her education; I said that the tone, the manners I adopted towards her, were those of good society, and proved the great esteem I entertained for her intelligence, but in the middle of all my fine speeches, towards the eleventh or twelfth day of my courtship, she suddenly put me out of all conceit by telling me that, being a priest, I ought to know that every amorous connection was a deadly sin, that God could see every action of His creatures, and that she would neither damn her soul nor place herself under the necessity of saying to her confessor that she had so far forgotten herself as to commit such a sin with a priest. I objected that I was not yet a priest, but she foiled me by enquiring point-blank whether or not the act I had in view was to be numbered amongst the cardinal sins, for, not feeling the courage to deny it, I felt that I must give up the argument and put an end to the adventure.

A little consideration having considerably calmed my feelings, everybody remarked my new countenance during dinner; and the old count, who was very fond of a joke, expressed loudly his opinion that such quiet demeanour on my part announced the complete success of my campaign. Considering such a remark to be favourable to me, I took care to spew my cruel devotee that such was the way the world would judge, but all this was lost labour. Luck, however, stood me in good stead, and my efforts were crowned with success in the following manner.

On Ascension Day, we all went to pay a visit to Madame Bergali, a celebrated Italian poetess. On my return to Pasean the same evening, my pretty mistress wished to get into a carriage for four persons in which her husband and sister were already seated, while I was alone in a two-wheeled chaise. I exclaimed at this, saying that such a mark of distrust was indeed too pointed, and everybody remonstrated with her, saying that she ought not to insult me so cruelly. She was compelled to come with me, and having told the postillion that I wanted to go by the nearest road, he left the other carriages, and took the way through the forest of Cequini. The sky was clear and cloudless when we left, but in less than half-an-hour we were visited by one of those storms so frequent in the south, which appear likely to overthrow heaven and earth, and which end rapidly, leaving behind them a bright sky and a cool atmosphere, so that they do more good than harm.

"Oh, heavens!" exclaimed my companion, "we shall have a storm."

"Yes," I say, "and although the chaise is covered, the rain will spoil your pretty dress. I am very sorry."

"I do not mind the dress; but the thunder frightens me so!"

"Close your ears."

"And the lightning?"

"Postillion, let us go somewhere for shelter."

"There is not a house, sir, for a league, and before we come to it, the storm will have passed off."

He quietly keeps on his way, and the lightning flashes, the thunder sends forth its mighty voice, and the lady shudders with fright. The rain comes down in torrents, I take off my cloak to shelter us in front, at the same moment we are blinded by a flash of lightning, and the electric fluid strikes the earth within one hundred yards of us. The horses plunge and prance with fear, and my companion falls in spasmodic convulsions. She throws herself upon me, and folds me in her arms. The cloak had gone down, I stoop to place it around us, and improving my opportunity I take up her clothes. She tries to pull them down, but another clap of thunder deprives her of every particle of strength. Covering her with the cloak, I draw her towards me, and the motion of the chaise coming to my assistance, she falls over me in the most favourable position. I lose no time, and under pretence of arranging my watch in my fob, I prepare myself for the assault. On her side, conscious that, unless she stops me at once, all is lost, she makes a great effort; but I hold her tightly, saying that if she does not feign a fainting fit, the post-boy will turn round and see everything; I let her enjoy the pleasure of calling me an infidel, a monster, anything she likes, but my victory is the most complete that ever a champion achieved.

The rain, however, was falling, the wind, which was very high, blew in our faces, and, compelled to stay where she was, she said I would ruin her reputation, as the postillion could see everything.

"I keep my eye upon him," I answered, "he is not thinking of us, and even if he should turn his head, the cloak shelters us from him. Be quiet, and pretend to have fainted, for I will not let you go."

She seems resigned, and asks how I can thus set the storm at defiance.

"The storm, dear one, is my best friend to-day."

She almost seems to believe me, her fear vanishes, and feeling my rapture, she enquires whether I have done. I smile and answer in the negative, stating that I cannot let her go till the storm is over. "Consent to everything, or I let the cloak drop," I say to her.

"Well, you dreadful man, are you satisfied, now that you have insured my misery for the remainder of my life?"

"No, not yet."

"What more do you want?"

"A shower of kisses."

"How unhappy I am! Well! here they are."

"Tell me you forgive me, and confess that you have shared all my pleasure."

"You know I did. Yes, I forgive you."

Then I give her her liberty, and treating her to some very pleasant caresses, I ask her to have the same kindness for me, and she goes to work with a smile on her pretty lips.

"Tell me you love me," I say to her.

"No, I do not, for you are an atheist, and hell awaits you."

The weather was fine again, and the elements calm; I kissed her hands and told her that the postillion had certainly not seen anything, and that I was sure I had cured her of her dread of thunder, but that she was not likely to reveal the secret of my remedy. She answered that one thing at least was certain, namely that no other woman had ever been cured by the same prescription.

"Why," I said, "the same remedy has very likely been applied a million of times within the last thousand years. To tell you the truth, I had somewhat depended upon it, when we entered the chaise together, for I did not know any other way of obtaining the happiness of possessing you. But console yourself with the belief that, placed in the same position, no frightened woman could have resisted."

"I believe you; but for the future I will travel only with my husband."

"You would be wrong, for your husband would not have been clever enough to cure your fright in the way I have done."

"True, again. One learns some curious things in your company; but we shall not travel tete-a-tete again."

We reached Pasean an hour before our friends. We get out of the chaise, and my fair mistress ran off to her chamber, while I was looking for a crown for the postillion. I saw that he was grinning.

"What are you laughing at?"

"Oh! you know."

"Here, take this ducat and keep a quiet tongue in your head."

CHAPTER VI

My Grandmother's Death and Its Consequences I Lose M. de Malipiero's
Friendship—I Have No Longer a Home—La Tintoretta—I Am Sent to a
Clerical Seminary—I Am Expelled From It, and Confined in a Fortress

During supper the conversation turned altogether upon the storm, and the official, who knew the weakness of his wife, told me that he was quite certain I would never travel with her again. "Nor I with him," his wife remarked, "for, in his fearful impiety, he exorcised the lightning with jokes."

Henceforth she avoided me so skilfully that I never could contrive another interview with her.

When I returned to Venice I found my grandmother ill, and I had to change all my habits, for I loved her too dearly not to surround her with every care and attention; I never left her until she had breathed her last. She was unable to leave me anything, for during her life she had given me all she could, and her death compelled me to adopt an entirely different mode of life.

A month after her death, I received a letter from my mother informing me that, as there was no probability of her return to Venice, she had determined to give up the house, the rent of which she was still paying, that she had communicated her intention to the Abbe Grimani, and that I was to be guided entirely by his advice.

He was instructed to sell the furniture, and to place me, as well as my brothers and my sister, in a good boarding-house. I called upon Grimani to assure him of my perfect disposition to obey his commands.

The rent of the house had been paid until the end of the year; but, as I was aware that the furniture would be sold on the expiration of the term, I placed my wants under no restraint. I had already sold some linen, most of the china, and several tapestries; I now began to dispose of the mirrors, beds, etc. I had no doubt that my conduct would be severely blamed, but I knew likewise that it was my father's inheritance, to which my mother had no claim whatever, and, as to my brothers, there was plenty of time before any explanation could take place between us.

Four months afterwards I had a second letter from my mother, dated from Warsaw, and enclosing another. Here is the translation of my mother's letter:

"My dear son, I have made here the acquaintance of a learned Minim friar, a Calabrian by birth, whose great qualities have made me think of you every time he has honoured me with a visit. A year ago I told him that I had a son who was preparing himself for the Church, but that I had not the means of keeping him during his studies, and he promised that my son would become his own child, if I could obtain for him from the queen a bishopric in his native country, and he added that it would be very easy to succeed if I could induce the sovereign to recommend him to her daughter, the queen of Naples.

"Full of trust in the Almighty, I threw myself at the feet of her majesty, who granted me her gracious protection. She wrote to her daughter, and the worthy friar has been appointed by the Pope to the bishopric of Monterano. Faithful to his promise, the good bishop will take you with him about the middle of next year, as he passes through Venice to reach Calabria. He informs you himself of his intentions in the enclosed letter. Answer him immediately, my dear son, and forward your letter to me; I will deliver it to the bishop. He will pave your way to the highest dignities of the Church, and you may imagine my consolation if, in some twenty or thirty years, I had the happiness of seeing you a bishop, at least! Until his arrival, M. Grimani will take care of you. I give you my blessing, and I am, my dear child, etc., etc."

The bishop's letter was written in Latin, and was only a repetition of my mother's. It was full of unction, and informed me that he would tarry but three days in Venice.

I answered according to my mother's wishes, but those two letters had turned my brain. I looked upon my fortune as made. I longed to enter the road which was to lead me to it, and I congratulated myself that I could leave my country without any regret. Farewell, Venice, I exclaimed; the days for vanity are gone by, and in the future I will only think of a great, of a substantial career! M. Grimani congratulated me warmly on my good luck, and promised all his friendly care to secure a good boarding-house, to which I would go at the beginning of the year, and where I would wait for the bishop's arrival.

M. de Malipiero, who in his own way had great wisdom, and who saw that in Venice I was plunging headlong into pleasures and dissipation, and was only wasting a precious time, was delighted to see me on the eve of going somewhere else to fulfil my destiny, and much pleased with my ready acceptance of those new circumstances in my life. He read me a lesson which I have never forgotten. "The famous precept of the Stoic philosophers," he said to me, "'Sequere Deum', can be perfectly explained by these words: 'Give yourself up to whatever fate offers to you, provided you do not feel an invincible repugnance to accept it.'" He added that it was the genius of Socrates, 'saepe revocans, raro impellens'; and that it was the origin of the 'fata viam inveniunt' of the same philosophers.

M. de Malipiero's science was embodied in that very lesson, for he had obtained his knowledge by the study of only one book—the book of man. However, as if it were to give me the proof that perfection does not exist, and that there is a bad side as well as a good one to everything, a certain adventure happened to me a month afterwards which, although I was following his own maxims, cost me the loss of his friendship, and which certainly did not teach me anything.

The senator fancied that he could trace upon the physiognomy of young people certain signs which marked them out as the special favourites of fortune. When he imagined that he had discovered those signs upon any individual, he would take him in hand and instruct him how to assist fortune by good and wise principles; and he used to say, with a great deal of truth, that a good remedy would turn into poison in the hands of a fool, but that poison is a good remedy when administered by a learned man. He had, in my time, three favourites in whose education he took great pains. They were, besides myself, Therese Imer, with whom the reader has a slight acquaintance already, and the third was the daughter of the boatman Gardela, a girl three years younger than I, who had the prettiest and most fascinating countenance. The speculative old man, in order to assist fortune in her particular case, made her learn dancing, for, he would say, the ball cannot reach the pocket unless someone pushes it. This girl made a great reputation at Stuttgard under the name of Augusta. She was the favourite mistress of the Duke of Wurtemburg in 1757. She was a most charming woman. The last time I saw her she was in Venice, and she died two years afterwards. Her husband, Michel de l'Agata, poisoned himself a short time after her death.

One day we had all three dined with him, and after dinner the senator left us, as was his wont, to enjoy his siesta; the little Gardela, having a dancing lesson to take, went away soon after him, and I found myself alone with Therese, whom I rather admired, although I had never made love to her. We were sitting down at a table very near each other, with our backs to the door of the room in which we thought our patron fast asleep, and somehow or other we took a fancy to examine into the difference of conformation between a girl and a boy; but at the most interesting part of our study a violent blow on my shoulders from a stick, followed by another, and which would have been itself followed by many more if I had not ran away, compelled us to abandon our interesting investigation unfinished. I got off without hat or cloak, and went home; but in less than a quarter of an hour the old housekeeper of the senator brought my clothes with a letter which contained a command never to present myself again at the mansion of his excellency. I immediately wrote him an answer in the following terms: "You have struck me while you were the slave of your anger; you cannot therefore boast of having given me a lesson, and I have not learned anything. To forgive you I must forget that you are a man of great wisdom, and I can never forget it."

This nobleman was perhaps quite right not to be pleased with the sight we gave him; yet, with all his prudence, he proved himself very unwise, for all the servants were acquainted with the cause of my exile, and, of course, the adventure was soon known through the city, and was received with great merriment. He dared not address any reproaches to Therese, as I heard from her soon after, but she could not venture to entreat him to pardon me.

The time to leave my father's house was drawing near, and one fine morning I received the visit of a man about forty years old, with a black wig, a scarlet cloak, and a very swarthy complexion, who handed me a letter from M. Grimani, ordering me to consign to the bearer all the furniture of the house according to the inventory, a copy of which was in my possession. Taking the inventory in my hand, I pointed out every article marked down, except when the said article, having through my instrumentality taken an airing out of the house, happened to be missing, and whenever any article was absent I said that I had not the slightest idea where it might be. But the uncouth fellow, taking a very high tone, said loudly that he must know what I had done with the furniture. His manner being very disagreeable to me, I answered that I had nothing to do with him, and as he still raised his voice I advised him to take himself off as quickly as possible, and I gave him that piece of advice in such a way as to prove to him that, at home, I knew I was the more powerful of the two.

Feeling it my duty to give information to M. Grimani of what had just taken place, I called upon him as soon as he was up, but I found that my man was already there, and that he had given his own account of the affair. The abbe, after a very severe lecture to which I had to listen in silence, ordered me to render an account of all the missing articles. I answered that I had found myself under the necessity of selling them to avoid running into debt. This confession threw him in a violent passion; he called me a rascal, said that those things did not belong to me, that he knew what he had to do, and he commanded me to leave his house on the very instant.

Mad with rage, I ran for a Jew, to whom I wanted to sell what remained of the furniture, but when I returned to my house I found a bailiff waiting at the door, and he handed me a summons. I looked over it and perceived that it was issued at the instance of Antonio Razetta. It was the name of the fellow with the swarthy countenance. The seals were already affixed on all the doors, and I was not even allowed to go to my room, for a keeper had been left there by the bailiff. I lost no time, and called upon M. Rosa, to whom I related all the circumstances. After reading the summons he said,

"The seals shall be removed to-morrow morning, and in the meantime I shall summon Razetta before the avogador. But to-night, my dear friend," he added, "you must beg the hospitality of some one of your acquaintances. It has been a violent proceeding, but you shall be paid handsomely for it; the man is evidently acting under M. Grimani's orders."

"Well, that is their business."

I spent the night with Nanette and Marton, and on the following morning, the seals having been taken off, I took possession of my dwelling. Razetta did not appear before the 'avogador', and M. Rosa summoned him in my name before the criminal court, and obtained against him a writ of 'capias' in case he should not obey the second summons. On the third day M. Grimani wrote to me, commanding me to call upon him. I went immediately. As soon as I was in his presence he enquired abruptly what my intentions were.

"I intend to shield myself from your violent proceedings under the protection of the law, and to defend myself against a man with whom I ought never to have had any connection, and who has compelled me to pass the night in a disreputable place."

"In a disreputable place?"

"Of course. Why was I, against all right and justice, prevented from entering my own dwelling?"

"You have possession of it now. But you must go to your lawyer and tell him to suspend all proceedings against Razetta, who has done nothing but under my instructions. I suspected that your intention was to sell the rest of the furniture; I have prevented it. There is a room at your disposal at St. Chrysostom's, in a house of mine, the first floor of which is occupied by La Tintoretta, our first opera dancer. Send all your things there, and come and dine with me every day. Your sister and your brothers have been provided with a comfortable home; therefore, everything is now arranged for the best."

I called at once upon M. Rosa, to whom I explained all that had taken place, and his advice being to give way to M. Grimani's wishes, I determined to follow it. Besides, the arrangement offered the best satisfaction I could obtain, as to be a guest at his dinner table was an honour for me. I was likewise full of curiosity respecting my new lodging under the same roof with La Tintoretta, who was much talked of, owing to a certain Prince of Waldeck who was extravagantly generous with her.

The bishop was expected in the course of the summer; I had, therefore, only six months more to wait in Venice before taking the road which would lead me, perhaps, to the throne of Saint Peter: everything in the future assumed in my eyes the brightest hue, and my imagination revelled amongst the most radiant beams of sunshine; my castles in the air were indeed most beautiful.

I dined the same day with M. Grimani, and I found myself seated next to Razetta—an unpleasant neighbour, but I took no notice of him. When the meal was over, I paid a last visit to my beautiful house in Saint-Samuel's parish, and sent all I possessed in a gondola to my new lodging.

I did not know Signora Tintoretta, but I was well acquainted with her reputation, character and manners. She was but a poor dancer, neither handsome nor plain, but a woman of wit and intellect. Prince Waldeck spent a great deal for her, and yet he did not prevent her from retaining the titulary protection of a noble Venetian of the Lin family, now extinct, a man about sixty years of age, who was her visitor at every hour of the day. This nobleman, who knew me, came to my room towards the evening, with the compliments of the lady, who, he added, was delighted to have me in her house, and would be pleased to receive me in her intimate circle.

To excuse myself for not having been the first to pay my respects to the signora, I told M. Lin that I did not know she was my neighbour, that M. Grimani had not mentioned the circumstance, otherwise I would have paid my duties to her before taking possession of my lodging. After this apology I followed the ambassador, he presented me to his mistress, and the acquaintance was made.

She received me like a princess, took off her glove before giving me her hand to kiss, mentioned my name before five or six strangers who were present, and whose names she gave me, and invited me to take a seat near her. As she was a native of Venice, I thought it was absurd for her to speak French to me, and I told her that I was not acquainted with that language, and would feel grateful if she would converse in Italian. She was surprised at my not speaking French, and said I would cut but a poor figure in her drawing-room, as they seldom spoke any other language there, because she received a great many foreigners. I promised to learn French.

Prince Waldeck came in during the evening; I was introduced to him, and he gave me a very friendly welcome. He could speak Italian very well, and during the carnival he chewed me great kindness. He presented me with a gold snuffbox as a reward for a very poor sonnet which I had written for his dear Grizellini. This was her family name; she was called Tintoretta because her father had been a dyer.

The Tintoretta had greater claims than Juliette to the admiration of sensible men. She loved poetry, and if it had not been that I was expecting the bishop, I would have fallen in love with her. She was herself smitten with a young physician of great merit, named Righelini, who died in the prime of life, and whom I still regret. I shall have to mention him in another part of my Memoirs.

Towards the end of the carnival, my mother wrote to M. Grimani that it would be a great shame if the bishop found me under the roof of an opera dancer, and he made up his mind to lodge me in a respectable and decent place. He took the Abbe Tosello into consultation, and the two gentlemen thought that the best thing they could do for me would be to send me to a clerical seminary. They arranged everything unknown to me, and the abbe undertook to inform me of their plan and to obtain from me a gracious consent. But when I heard him speak with beautiful flowers of rhetoric for the purpose of gilding the bitter pill, I could not help bursting into a joyous laughter, and I astounded his reverence when I expressed my readiness to go anywhere he might think right to send me.

The plan of the two worthy gentlemen was absurd, for at the age of seventeen, and with a nature like mine, the idea of placing me in a seminary ought never to have been entertained, but ever a faithful disciple of Socrates, feeling no unconquerable reluctance, and the plan, on the contrary, appearing to me rather a good joke, I not only gave a ready consent, but I even longed to enter the seminary. I told M. Grimani I was prepared to accept anything, provided Razetta had nothing to do with it. He gave me his promise, but he did not keep it when I left the seminary. I have never been able to decide whether this Grimani was kind because he was a fool, or whether his stupidity was the result of his kindness, but all his brothers were the same. The worst trick that Dame Fortune can play upon an intelligent young man is to place him under the dependence of a fool. A few days afterwards, having been dressed as a pupil of a clerical seminary by the care of the abbe, I was taken to Saint-Cyprian de Muran and introduced to the rector.

The patriarchal church of Saint-Cyprian is served by an order of the monks, founded by the blessed Jerome Miani, a nobleman of Venice. The rector received me with tender affection and great kindness. But in his address (which was full of unction) I thought I could perceive a suspicion on his part that my being sent to the seminary was a punishment, or at least a way to put a stop to an irregular life, and, feeling hurt in my dignity, I told him at once, "Reverend father, I do not think that any one has the right of punishing me."

"No, no, my son," he answered, "I only meant that you would be very happy with us."

We were then shewn three halls, in which we found at least one hundred and fifty seminarists, ten or twelve schoolrooms, the refectory, the dormitory, the gardens for play hours, and every pain was taken to make me imagine life in such a place the happiest that could fall to the lot of a young man, and to make me suppose that I would even regret the arrival of the bishop. Yet they all tried to cheer me up by saying that I would only remain there five or six months. Their eloquence amused me greatly.

I entered the seminary at the beginning of March, and prepared myself for my new life by passing the night between my two young friends, Nanette and Marton, who bathed their pillows with tears; they could not understand, and this was likewise the feeling of their aunt and of the good M. Rosa, how a young man like myself could shew such obedience.

The day before going to the seminary, I had taken care to entrust all my papers to Madame Manzoni. They made a large parcel, and I left it in her hands for fifteen years. The worthy old lady is still alive, and with her ninety years she enjoys good health and a cheerful temper. She received me with a smile, and told me that I would not remain one month in the seminary.

"I beg your pardon, madam, but I am very glad to go there, and intend to remain until the arrival of the bishop."

"You do not know your own nature, and you do not know your bishop, with whom you will not remain very long either."

The abbe accompanied me to the seminary in a gondola, but at Saint-Michel he had to stop in consequence of a violent attack of vomiting which seized me suddenly; the apothecary cured me with some mint-water.

I was indebted for this attack to the too frequent sacrifices which I had been offering on the altar of love. Any lover who knows what his feelings were when he found himself with the woman he adored and with the fear that it was for the last time, will easily imagine my feelings during the last hours that I expected ever to spend with my two charming mistresses. I could not be induced to let the last offering be the last, and I went on offering until there was no more incense left.

The priest committed me to the care of the rector, and my luggage was carried to the dormitory, where I went myself to deposit my cloak and my hat. I was not placed amongst the adults, because, notwithstanding my size, I was not old enough. Besides, I would not shave myself, through vanity, because I thought that the down on my face left no doubt of my youth. It was ridiculous, of course; but when does man cease to be so? We get rid of our vices more easily than of our follies. Tyranny has not had sufficient power over me to compel me to shave myself; it is only in that respect that I have found tyranny to be tolerant.

"To which school do you wish to belong?" asked the rector.

"To the dogmatic, reverend father; I wish to study the history of the Church."

"I will introduce you to the father examiner."

"I am doctor in divinity, most reverend father, and do not want to be examined."

"It is necessary, my dear son; come with me."

This necessity appeared to me an insult, and I felt very angry; but a spirit of revenge quickly whispered to me the best way to mystify them, and the idea made me very joyful. I answered so badly all the questions propounded in Latin by the examiner, I made so many solecisms, that he felt it his duty to send me to an inferior class of grammar, in which, to my great delight, I found myself the companion of some twenty young urchins of about ten years, who, hearing that I was doctor in divinity, kept on saying: 'Accipiamus pecuniam, et mittamus asinum in patriam suam'.

Our play hours afforded me great amusement; my companions of the dormitory, who were all in the class of philosophy at least, looked down upon me with great contempt, and when they spoke of their own sublime discourses, they laughed if I appeared to be listening attentively to their discussions which, as they thought, must have been perfect enigmas to me. I did not intend to betray myself, but an accident, which I could not avoid, forced me to throw off the mask.

Father Barbarigo, belonging to the Convent of the Salutation at Venice, whose pupil I had been in physics, came to pay a visit to the rector, and seeing me as we were coming from mass paid me his friendly compliments. His first question was to enquire what science I was studying, and he thought I was joking when I answered that I was learning the grammar. The rector having joined us, I left them together, and went to my class. An our later, the rector sent for me.

"Why did you feign such ignorance at the examination?" he asked.

"Why," I answered, "were you unjust enough to compel me to the degradation of an examination?"

He looked annoyed, and escorted me to the dogmatic school, where my comrades of the dormitory received me with great astonishment, and in the afternoon, at play time, they gathered around me and made me very happy with their professions of friendship.

One of them, about fifteen years old, and who at the present time must, if still alive, be a bishop, attracted my notice by his features as much as by his talents. He inspired me with a very warm friendship, and during recess, instead of playing skittles with the others, we always walked together. We conversed upon poetry, and we both delighted in the beautiful odes of Horace. We liked Ariosto better than Tasso, and Petrarch had our whole admiration, while Tassoni and Muratori, who had been his critics, were the special objects of our contempt. We were such fast friends, after four days of acquaintance, that we were actually jealous of each other, and to such an extent that if either of us walked about with any seminarist, the other would be angry and sulk like a disappointed lover.

The dormitory was placed under the supervision of a lay friar, and it was his province to keep us in good order. After supper, accompanied by this lay friar, who had the title of prefect, we all proceeded to the dormitory. There, everyone had to go to his own bed, and to undress quietly after having said his prayers in a low voice. When all the pupils were in bed, the prefect would go to his own. A large lantern lighted up the dormitory, which had the shape of a parallelogram eighty yards by ten. The beds were placed at equal distances, and to each bed there were a fold-stool, a chair, and room for the trunk of the Seminarist. At one end was the washing place, and at the other the bed of the prefect. The bed of my friend was opposite mine, and the lantern was between us.

The principal duty of the prefect was to take care that no pupil should go and sleep with one of his comrades, for such a visit was never supposed an innocent one. It was a cardinal sin, and, bed being accounted the place for sleep and not for conversation, it was admitted that a pupil who slept out of his own bed, did so only for immoral purposes. So long as he stopped in his own bed, he could do what he liked; so much the worse for him if he gave himself up to bad practices. It has been remarked in Germany that it is precisely in those institutions for young men in which the directors have taken most pains to prevent onanism that this vice is most prevalent.

Those who had framed the regulations in our seminary were stupid fools, who had not the slightest knowledge of either morals or human nature. Nature has wants which must be administered to, and Tissot is right only as far as the abuse of nature is concerned, but this abuse would very seldom occur if the directors exercised proper wisdom and prudence, and if they did not make a point of forbidding it in a special and peculiar manner; young people give way to dangerous excesses from a sheer delight in disobedience,—a disposition very natural to humankind, since it began with Adam and Eve.

I had been in the seminary for nine or ten days, when one night I felt someone stealing very quietly in my bed; my hand was at once clutched, and my name whispered. I could hardly restrain my laughter. It was my friend, who, having chanced to wake up and finding that the lantern was out, had taken a sudden fancy to pay me a visit. I very soon begged him to go away for fear the prefect should be awake, for in such a case we should have found ourselves in a very unpleasant dilemma, and most likely would have been accused of some abominable offence. As I was giving him that good advice we heard someone moving, and my friend made his escape; but immediately after he had left me I heard the fall of some person, and at the same time the hoarse voice of the prefect exclaiming:

"Ah, villain! wait until to-morrow—until to-morrow!"

After which threat he lighted the lantern and retired to his couch.

The next morning, before the ringing of the bell for rising, the rector, followed by the prefect, entered the dormitory, and said to us:

"Listen to me, all of you. You are aware of what has taken place this last night. Two amongst you must be guilty; but I wish to forgive them, and to save their honour I promise that their names shall not be made public. I expect every one of you to come to me for confession before recess."

He left the dormitory, and we dressed ourselves. In the afternoon, in obedience to his orders, we all went to him and confessed, after which ceremony we repaired to the garden, where my friend told me that, having unfortunately met the prefect after he left me, he had thought that the best way was to knock him down, in order to get time to reach his own bed without being known.

"And now," I said, "you are certain of being forgiven, for, of course, you have wisely confessed your error?"

"You are joking," answered my friend; "why, the good rector would not have known any more than he knows at present, even if my visit to you had been paid with a criminal intent."

"Then you must have made a false confession: you are at all events guilty of disobedience?"

"That may be, but the rector is responsible for the guilt, as he used compulsion."

"My dear friend, you argue in a very forcible way, and the very reverend rector must by this time be satisfied that the inmates of our dormitory are more learned than he is himself."

195

No more would have been said about the adventure if, a few nights after, I had not in my turn taken a fancy to return the visit paid by my friend. Towards midnight, having had occasion to get out of bed, and hearing the loud snoring of the prefect, I quickly put out the lantern and went to lie beside my friend. He knew me at once, and gladly received me; but we both listened attentively to the snoring of our keeper, and when it ceased, understanding our danger, I got up and reached my own bed without losing a second, but the moment I got to it I had a double surprise. In the first place I felt somebody lying in my bed, and in the second I saw the prefect, with a candle in his hand, coming along slowly and taking a survey of all the beds right and left. I could understand the prefect suddenly lighting a candle, but how could I realize what I saw—namely, one of my comrades sleeping soundly in my bed, with his back turned to me? I immediately made up my mind to feign sleep. After two or three shakings given by the prefect, I pretended to wake up, and my bed-companion woke up in earnest. Astonished at finding himself in my bed, he offered me an apology:

"I have made a mistake," he said, "as I returned from a certain place in the dark, I found your bed empty, and mistook it for mine."

"Very likely," I answered; "I had to get up, too."

"Yes," remarked the prefect; "but how does it happen that you went to bed without making any remark when, on your return, you found your bed already tenanted? And how is it that, being in the dark, you did not suppose that you were mistaken yourself?"

"I could not be mistaken, for I felt the pedestal of this crucifix of mine, and I knew I was right; as to my companion here, I did not feel him."

"It is all very unlikely," answered our Argus; and he went to the lantern, the wick of which he found crushed down.

"The wick has been forced into the oil, gentlemen; it has not gone out of itself; it has been the handiwork of one of you, but it will be seen to in the morning."

My stupid companion went to his own bed, the prefect lighted the lamp and retired to his rest, and after this scene, which had broken the repose of every pupil, I quietly slept until the appearance of the rector, who, at the dawn of day, came in great fury, escorted by his satellite, the prefect.

The rector, after examining the localities and submitting to a lengthy interrogatory first my accomplice, who very naturally was considered as the most guilty, and then myself, whom nothing could convict of the offence, ordered us to get up and go to church to attend mass. As soon as we were dressed, he came back, and addressing us both, he said, kindly:

"You stand both convicted of a scandalous connivance, and it is proved by the fact of the lantern having been wilfully extinguished. I am disposed to believe that the cause of all this disorder is, if not entirely innocent, at least due only to extreme thoughtlessness; but the scandal given to all your comrades, the outrage offered to the discipline and to the established rules of the seminary, call loudly for punishment. Leave the room."

We obeyed; but hardly were we between the double doors of the dormitory than we were seized by four servants, who tied our hands behind us, and led us to the class room, where they compelled us to kneel down before the great crucifix. The rector told them to execute his orders, and, as we were in that position, the wretches administered to each of us seven or eight blows with a stick, or with a rope, which I received, as well as my companion, without a murmur. But the moment my hands were free, I asked the rector whether I could write two lines at the very foot of the cross. He gave orders to bring ink and paper, and I traced the following words:

"I solemnly swear by this God that I have never spoken to the seminarist who was found in my bed. As an innocent person I must protest against this shameful violence. I shall appeal to the justice of his lordship the patriarch."

My comrade in misery signed this protest with me; after which, addressing myself to all the pupils, I read it aloud, calling upon them to speak the truth if any one could say the contrary of what I had written. They, with one voice, immediately declared that we had never been seen conversing together, and that no one knew who had put the lamp out. The rector left the room in the midst of hisses and curses, but he sent us to prison all the same at the top of the house and in separate cells. An hour afterwards, I had my bed, my trunk and all my things, and my meals were brought to me every day. On the fourth day, the Abbe Tosello came for me with instructions to bring me to Venice. I asked him whether he had sifted this unpleasant affair; he told me that he had enquired into it, that he had seen the other seminarist, and that he believed we were both innocent; but the rector would not confess himself in the wrong, and he did not see what could be done.

I threw off my seminarist's habit, and dressed myself in the clothes I used to wear in Venice, and, while my luggage was carried to a boat, I accompanied the abbe to M. Grimani's gondola in which he had come, and we took our departure. On our way, the abbe ordered the boatman to leave my things at the Palace Grimani, adding that he was instructed by M. Grimani to tell me that, if I had the audacity to present myself at his mansion, his servants had received orders to turn me away.

He landed me near the convent of the Jesuits, without any money, and with nothing but what I had on my back.

I went to beg a dinner from Madame Manzoni, who laughed heartily at the realization of her prediction. After dinner I called upon M. Rosa to see whether the law could protect me against the tyranny of my enemies, and after he had been made acquainted with the circumstances of the case, he promised to bring me the same evening, at Madame Orio's house, an extra-judicial act. I repaired to the place of appointment to wait for him, and to enjoy the pleasure of my two charming friends at my sudden reappearance. It was indeed very great, and the recital of my adventures did not astonish them less than my unexpected presence. M. Rosa came and made me read the act which he had prepared; he had not had time to have it engrossed by the notary, but he undertook to have it ready the next day.

I left Madame Orio to take supper with my brother Francois, who resided with a painter called Guardi; he was, like me, much oppressed by the tyranny of Grimani, and I promised to deliver him. Towards midnight I returned to the two amiable sisters who were expecting me with their usual loving impatience, but, I am bound to confess it with all humility, my sorrows were prejudicial to love in spite of the fortnight of absence and of abstinence. They were themselves deeply affected to see me so unhappy, and pitied me with all their hearts. I endeavoured to console them, and assured them that all my misery would soon come to an end, and that we would make up for lost time.

In the morning, having no money, and not knowing where to go, I went to St. Mark's Library, where I remained until noon. I left it with the intention of dining with Madame Manzoni, but I was suddenly accosted by a soldier who informed me that someone wanted to speak to me in a gondola to which he pointed. I answered that the person might as well come out, but he quietly remarked that he had a friend at hand to conduct me forcibly to the gondola, if necessary, and without any more hesitation I went towards it. I had a great dislike to noise or to anything like a public exhibition. I might have resisted, for the soldiers were unarmed, and I would not have been taken up, this sort of arrest not being legal in Venice, but I did not think of it. The 'sequere deum' was playing its part; I felt no reluctance. Besides, there are moments in which a courageous man has no courage, or disdains to shew it.

I enter the gondola, the curtain is drawn aside, and I see my evil genius, Razetta, with an officer. The two soldiers sit down at the prow; I recognize M. Grimani's own gondola, it leaves the landing and takes the direction of the Lido. No one spoke to me, and I remained silent. After half-an-hour's sailing, the gondola stopped before the small entrance of the Fortress St. Andre, at the mouth of the Adriatic, on the very spot where the Bucentaur stands, when, on Ascension Day, the doge comes to espouse the sea.

The sentinel calls the corporal; we alight, the officer who accompanied me introduces me to the major, and presents a letter to him. The major, after reading its contents, gives orders to M. Zen, his adjutant, to consign me to the guard-house. In another quarter of an hour my conductors take their departure, and M.

Zen brings me three livres and a half, stating that I would receive the same amount every week. It was exactly the pay of a private.

I did not give way to any burst of passion, but I felt the most intense indignation. Late in the evening I expressed a wish to have some food bought, for I could not starve; then, stretching myself upon a hard camp bed, I passed the night amongst the soldiers without closing my eyes, for these Sclavonians were singing, eating garlic, smoking a bad tobacco which was most noxious, and drinking a wine of their own country, as black as ink, which nobody else could swallow.

Early next morning Major Pelodoro (the governor of the fortress) called me up to his room, and told me that, in compelling me to spend the night in the guard-house, he had only obeyed the orders he had received from Venice from the secretary of war. "Now, reverend sir," he added, "my further orders are only to keep you a prisoner in the fort, and I am responsible for your remaining here. I give you the whole of the fortress for your prison. You shall have a good room in which you will find your bed and all your luggage. Walk anywhere you please; but recollect that, if you should escape, you would cause my ruin. I am sorry that my instructions are to give you only ten sous a day, but if you have any friends in Venice able to send you some money, write to them, and trust to me for the security of your letters. Now you may go to bed, if you need rest."

I was taken to my room; it was large and on the first story, with two windows from which I had a very fine view. I found my bed, and I ascertained with great satisfaction that my trunk, of which I had the keys, had not been forced open. The major had kindly supplied my table with all the implements necessary for writing. A Sclavonian soldier informed me very politely that he would attend upon me, and that I would pay him for his services whenever I could, for everyone knew that I had only ten sous a day. I began by ordering some soup, and, when I had dispatched it, I went to bed and slept for nine hours. When I woke, I received an invitation to supper from the major, and I began to imagine that things, after all, would not be so very bad.

I went to the honest governor, whom I found in numerous company. He presented me to his wife and to every person present. I met there several officers, the chaplain of the fortress, a certain Paoli Vida, one of the singers of St. Mark's Church, and his wife, a pretty woman, sister-in-law of the major, whom the husband chose to confine in the fort because he was very jealous (jealous men are not comfortable at Venice), together with several other ladies, not very young, but whom I thought very agreeable, owing to their kind welcome.

Cheerful as I was by nature, those pleasant guests easily managed to put me in the best of humours. Everyone expressed a wish to know the reasons which could have induced M. Grimani to send me to the fortress, so I gave a faithful account of all my adventures since my grandmother's death. I spoke for three hours without any bitterness, and even in a pleasant tone, upon things which, said in a different manner, might have displeased my audience; all expressed their satisfaction, and shewed so much sympathy that, as we parted for the night, I received from all an assurance of friendship and the offer of their services. This is a piece of good fortune which has never failed me whenever I have been the victim of oppression, until I reached the age of fifty. Whenever I met with honest persons expressing a curiosity to know the history of the misfortune under which I was labouring, and whenever I satisfied their curiosity, I have inspired them with friendship, and with that sympathy which was necessary to render them favourable and useful to me.

That success was owing to a very simple artifice; it was only to tell my story in a quiet and truthful manner, without even avoiding the facts which told against me. It is simple secret that many men do not know, because the larger portion of humankind is composed of cowards; a man who always tells the truth must be possessed of great moral courage. Experience has taught me that truth is a talisman, the charm of which never fails in its effect, provided it is not wasted upon unworthy people, and I believe that a guilty man, who candidly speaks the truth to his judge, has a better chance of being acquitted, than the innocent man who hesitates and evades true statements. Of course the speaker must be young, or at least in the prime of manhood; for an old man finds the whole of nature combined against him.

The major had his joke respecting the visit paid and returned to the seminarist's bed, but the chaplain and the ladies scolded him. The major advised me to write out my story and send it to the secretary of war, undertaking that he should receive it, and he assured me that he would become my protector. All the ladies tried to induce me to follow the major's advice.

CHAPTER VII

The fort, in which the Republic usually kept only a garrison of one hundred half-pay Sclavonians, happened to contain at that time two thousand Albanian soldiers, who were called Cimariotes.

The secretary of war, who was generally known under the title of 'sage a l'ecriture', had summoned these men from the East in consequence of some impending promotion, as he wanted the officers to be on the spot in order to prove their merits before being rewarded. They all came from the part of Epirus called Albania, which belongs to the Republic of Venice, and they had distinguished themselves in the last war against the Turks. It was for me a new and extraordinary sight to examine some eighteen or twenty officers, all of an advanced age, yet strong and healthy, shewing the scars which covered their face and their chest, the last naked and entirely exposed through military pride. The lieutenant-colonel was particularly conspicuous by his wounds, for, without exaggeration, he had lost one-fourth of his head. He had but one eye, but one ear, and no jaw to speak of. Yet he could eat very well, speak without difficulty, and was very cheerful. He had with him all his family, composed of two pretty daughters, who looked all the prettier in their national costume, and of seven sons, every one of them a soldier. This lieutenant-colonel stood six feet high, and his figure was magnificent, but his scars so completely deformed his features that his face was truly horrid to look at. Yet I found so much attraction in him that I liked him the moment I saw him, and I would have been much pleased to converse with him if his breath had not sent forth such a strong smell of garlic. All the Albanians had their pockets full of it, and they enjoyed a piece of garlic with as much relish as we do a sugar-plum. After this none can maintain it to be a poison, though the only medicinal virtue it possesses is to excite the appetite, because it acts like a tonic upon a weak stomach.

The lieutenant-colonel could not read, but he was not ashamed of his ignorance, because not one amongst his men, except the priest and the surgeon, could boast greater learning. Every man, officer or private, had his purse full of gold; half of them, at least, were married, and we had in the fortress a colony of five or six hundred women, with God knows how many children! I felt greatly interested in them all. Happy idleness! I often regret thee because thou hast often offered me new sights, and for the same reason I hate old age which never offers but what I know already, unless I should take up a gazette, but I cared nothing for them in my young days.

Alone in my room I made an inventory of my trunk, and having put aside everything of an ecclesiastical character, I sent for a Jew, and sold the whole parcel unmercifully. Then I wrote to M. Rosa, enclosing all the tickets of the articles I had pledged, requesting him to have them sold without any exception, and to forward me the surplus raised by the sale. Thanks to that double operation, I was enabled to give my Sclavonian servant the ten sous allowed to me every day. Another soldier, who had been a hair-dresser, took care of my hair which I had been compelled to neglect, in consequence of the rules of the seminary. I spent my time in walking about the fort and through the barracks, and my two places of resort were the major's apartment for some intellectual enjoyment, and the rooms of the Albanian lieutenant-colonel for a sprinkling of love. The Albanian feeling certain that his colonel would be appointed brigadier, solicited the command of the regiment, but he had a rival and he feared his success. I wrote him a petition, short, but so well composed that the secretary of war, having enquired the name of the author, gave the Albanian his colonelcy. On his return to the fort, the brave fellow, overjoyed at his success, hugged me in his arms, saying that he owed it all to me; he invited me to a family dinner, in which my very soul was parched by his garlic, and he presented me with twelve botargoes and two pounds of excellent Turkish tobacco.

The result of my petition made all the other officers think that they could not succeed without the assistance of my pen, and I willingly gave it to everybody; this entailed many quarrels upon me, for I served all interests, but, finding myself the lucky possessor of some forty sequins, I was no longer in dread of poverty, and laughed at everything. However, I met with an accident which made me pass six weeks in a very unpleasant condition.

On the 2nd of April, the fatal anniversary of my first appearance in this world, as I was getting up in the morning, I received in my room the visit of a very handsome Greek woman, who told me that her husband, then ensign in the regiment, had every right to claim the rank of lieutenant, and that he would certainly be appointed, if it were not for the opposition of his captain who was against him, because she had refused him certain favours which she could bestow only upon her husband. She handed me some certificates, and begged me to write a petition which she would present herself to the secretary of war, adding that she could only offer me her heart in payment. I answered that her heart ought not to go alone; I acted as I had spoken, and I met with no other resistance than the objection which a pretty woman is always sure to feign for the sake of appearance. After that, I told her to come back at noon, and that the petition would be ready. She was exact to the appointment, and very kindly rewarded me a second time; and in the evening, under pretence of some alterations to be made in the petition, she afforded an excellent opportunity of reaping a third recompense.

But, alas! the path of pleasure is not strewn only with roses! On the third day, I found out, much to my dismay, that a serpent had been hid under the flowers. Six weeks of care and of rigid diet re-established my health.

When I met the handsome Greek again, I was foolish enough to reproach her for the present she had bestowed upon me, but she baffled me by laughing, and saying that she had only offered me what she possessed, and that it was my own fault if I had not been sufficiently careful. The reader cannot imagine how much this first misfortune grieved me, and what deep shame I felt. I looked upon myself as a dishonoured man, and while I am on that subject I may as well relate an incident which will give some idea of my thoughtlessness.

Madame Vida, the major's sister-in-law, being alone with me one morning, confided in me in a moment of unreserved confidence what she had to suffer from the jealous disposition of her husband, and his cruelty in having allowed her to sleep alone for the last four years, when she was in the very flower of her age.

"I trust to God," she added, "that my husband will not find out that you have spent an hour alone with me, for I should never hear the end of it."

Feeling deeply for her grief, and confidence begetting confidence, I was stupid enough to tell her the sad state to which I had been reduced by the cruel Greek woman, assuring her that I felt my misery all the more deeply, because I should have been delighted to console her, and to give her the opportunity of a revenge for her jealous husband's coldness. At this speech, in which my simplicity and good faith could easily be traced, she rose from her chair, and upbraided me with every insult which an outraged honest woman might hurl at the head of a bold libertine who has presumed too far. Astounded, but understanding perfectly well the nature of my crime, I bowed myself out of her room; but as I was leaving it she told me in the same angry tone that my visits would not be welcome for the future, as I was a conceited puppy, unworthy of the society of good and respectable women. I took care to answer that a respectable woman would have been rather more reserved than she had been in her confidences. On reflection I felt pretty sure that, if I had been in good health, or had said nothing about my mishap, she would have been but too happy to receive my consolations.

A few days after that incident I had a much greater cause to regret my acquaintance with the Greek woman. On Ascension Day, as the ceremony of the Bucentaur was celebrated near the fort, M. Rosa brought Madame Orio and her two nieces to witness it, and I had the pleasure of treating them all to a good dinner in my room. I found myself, during the day, alone with my young friends in one of the casements, and they both loaded me with the most loving caresses and kisses. I felt that they expected some substantial proof of my love; but, to conceal the real state, of things, I pretended to be afraid of being surprised, and they had to be satisfied with my shallow excuse.

I had informed my mother by letter of all I had suffered from Grimani's treatment; she answered that she had written to him on the subject, that she had no doubt he would immediately set me at liberty, and that an arrangement had been entered into by which M. Grimani would devote the money raised by Razetta from the sale of the furniture to the settlement of a small patrimony on my youngest brother. But in this matter Grimani did not act honestly, for the patrimony was only settled thirteen years afterwards, and even then only in a fictitious manner. I shall have an opportunity later on of mentioning this unfortunate brother, who died very poor in Rome twenty years ago.

Towards the middle of June the Cimariotes were sent back to the East, and after their departure the garrison of the fort was reduced to its usual number. I began to feel weary in this comparative solitude, and I gave way to terrible fits of passion.

The heat was intense, and so disagreeable to me that I wrote to M. Grimani, asking for two summer suits of clothes, and telling him where they would be found, if Razetta had not sold them. A week afterwards I was in the major's apartment when I saw the wretch Razetta come in, accompanied by a man whom he introduced as Petrillo, the celebrated favourite of the Empress of Russia, just arrived from St. Petersburg. He ought to have said infamous instead of celebrated, and clown instead of favourite.

The major invited them to take a seat, and Razetta, receiving a parcel from Grimani's gondolier, handed it to me, saying,

"I have brought you your rags; take them."

I answered:

"Some day I will bring you a 'rigano':"

At these words the scoundrel dared to raise his cane, but the indignant major compelled him to lower his tone by asking him whether he had any wish to pass the night in the guard-house. Petrillo, who had not yet opened his lips, told me then that he was sorry not to have found me in Venice, as I might have shewn him round certain places which must be well known to me.

"Very likely we should have met your wife in such places," I answered.

"I am a good judge of faces," he said, "and I can see that you are a true gallows-bird."

I was trembling with rage, and the major, who shared my utter disgust, told them that he had business to transact, and they took their leave. The major assured me that on the following day he would go to the war office to complain of Razetta, and that he would have him punished for his insolence.

I remained alone, a prey to feelings of the deepest indignation, and to a most ardent thirst for revenge.

The fortress was entirely surrounded by water, and my windows were not overlooked by any of the sentinels. A boat coming under my windows could therefore easily take me to Venice during the night and bring me back to the fortress before day-break. All that was necessary was to find a boatman who, for a certain amount, would risk the galleys in case of discovery. Amongst several who brought provisions to the fort, I chose a boatman whose countenance pleased me, and I offered him one sequin; he promised to let me know his decision on the following day. He was true to his time, and declared himself ready to take me. He informed me that, before deciding to serve me, he had wished to know whether I was kept in the fort for any great crime, but as the wife of the major had told him that my imprisonment had been caused by very trifling frolics, I could rely upon him. We arranged that he should be under my window at the beginning of the night, and that his boat should be provided with a mast long enough to enable me to slide along it from the window to the boat.

The appointed hour came, and everything being ready I got safely into the boat, landed at the Sclavonian quay, ordered the boatman to wait for me, and wrapped up in a mariner's cloak I took my way straight to the gate of Saint-Sauveur, and engaged the waiter of a coffee-room to take me to Razetta's house.

Being quite certain that he would not be at home at that time, I rang the bell, and I heard my sister's voice telling me that if I wanted to see him I must call in the morning. Satisfied with this, I went to the foot of the bridge and sat down, waiting there to see which way he would come, and a few minutes before midnight I saw him advancing from the square of Saint-Paul. It was all I wanted to know; I went back to my boat and returned to the fort without any difficulty. At five o'clock in the morning everyone in the garrison could see me enjoying my walk on the platform.

Taking all the time necessary to mature my plans, I made the following arrangements to secure my revenge with perfect safety, and to prove an alibi in case I should kill my rascally enemy, as it was my intention to do. The day preceding the night fixed for my expedition, I walked about with the son of the Adjutant Zen, who was only twelve years old, but who amused me much by his shrewdness. The reader will meet him again in the year 1771. As I was walking with him, I jumped down from one of the bastions, and feigned to sprain my ankle. Two soldiers carried me to my room, and the surgeon of the fort, thinking that I was suffering from a luxation, ordered me to keep to bed, and wrapped up the ankle in towels saturated with camphorated spirits of wine. Everybody came to see me, and I requested the soldier who served me to remain and to sleep in my room. I knew that a glass of brandy was enough to stupefy the man, and to make him sleep soundly. As soon as I saw him fast asleep, I begged the surgeon and the chaplain, who had his room over mine, to leave me, and at half-past ten I lowered myself in the boat.

As soon as I reached Venice, I bought a stout cudgel, and I sat myself down on a door-step, at the corner of the street near Saint-Paul's Square. A narrow canal at the end of the street, was, I thought, the very place to throw my enemy in. That canal has now disappeared.

At a quarter before twelve I see Razetta, walking along leisurely. I come out of the street with rapid strides, keeping near the wall to compel him to make room for me, and I strike a first blow on the head, and a second on his arm; the third blow sends him tumbling in the canal, howling and screaming my name. At the same instant a Forlan, or citizen of Forli, comes out of a house on my left side with a lantern in his hand. A blow from my cudgel knocks the lantern out of his grasp, and the man, frightened out of his wits, takes to his heels. I throw away my stick, I run at full speed through the square and over the bridge, and while people are hastening towards the spot where the disturbance had taken place, I jump into the boat, and, thanks to a strong breeze swelling our sail, I get back to the fortress. Twelve o'clock was striking as I re-entered my room through the window. I quickly undress myself, and the moment I am in my bed I wake up the soldier by my loud screams, telling him to go for the surgeon, as I am dying of the colic.

The chaplain, roused by my screaming, comes down and finds me in convulsions. In the hope that some diascordium would relieve me, the good old man runs to his room and brings it, but while he has gone for some water I hide the medicine. After half an hour of wry faces, I say that I feel much better, and thanking all my friends, I beg them to retire, which everyone does, wishing me a quiet sleep.

The next morning I could not get up in consequence of my sprained ankle, although I had slept very well; the major was kind enough to call upon me before going to Venice, and he said that very likely my colic had been caused by the melon I had eaten for my dinner the day before.

The major returned at one o'clock in the afternoon. "I have good news to give you," he said to me, with a joyful laugh. "Razetta was soundly cudgelled last night and thrown into a canal."

"Has he been killed?"

"No; but I am glad of it for your sake, for his death would make your position much more serious. You are accused of having done it."

"I am very glad people think me guilty; it is something of a revenge, but it will be rather difficult to bring it home to me."

"Very difficult! All the same, Razetta swears he recognized you, and the same declaration is made by the Forlan who says that you struck his hand to make him drop his lantern. Razetta's nose is broken, three of his teeth are gone, and his right arm is severely hurt. You have been accused before the avogador, and M. Grimani has written to the war office to complain of your release from the fortress without his knowledge. I arrived at the office just in time. The secretary was reading Grimani's letter, and I assured his excellency that it was a false report, for I left you in bed this morning, suffering from a sprained ankle. I told him likewise that at twelve o'clock last night you were very near death from a severe attack of colic."

"Was it at midnight that Razetta was so well treated?"

"So says the official report. The war secretary wrote at once to M. Grimani and informed him that you have not left the fort, and that you are even now detained in it, and that the plaintiff is at liberty, if he chooses, to send commissaries to ascertain the fact. Therefore, my dear abbe, you must prepare yourself for an interrogatory."

"I expect it, and I will answer that I am very sorry to be innocent."

Three days afterwards, a commissary came to the fort with a clerk of the court, and the proceedings were soon over. Everybody knew that I had sprained my ankle; the chaplain, the surgeon, my body-servant, and several others swore that at midnight I was in bed suffering from colic. My alibi being thoroughly proved, the avogador sentenced Razetta and the Forlan to pay all expenses without prejudice to my rights of action.

After this judgment, the major advised me to address to the secretary of war a petition which he undertook to deliver himself, and to claim my release from the fort. I gave notice of my proceedings to M. Grimani, and a week afterwards the major told me that I was free, and that he would himself take me to the abbe. It was at dinnertime, and in the middle of some amusing conversation, that he imparted that piece of information. Not supposing him to be in earnest, and in order to keep up the joke, I told him very politely that I preferred his house to Venice, and that, to prove it, I would be happy to remain a week longer, if he would grant me permission to do so. I was taken at my word, and everybody seemed very pleased. But when, two hours later, the news was confirmed, and I could no longer doubt the truth of my release, I repented the week which I had so foolishly thrown away as a present to the major; yet I had not the courage to break my word, for everybody, and particularly his wife, had shown such unaffected pleasure, it would have been contemptible of me to change my mind. The good woman knew that I owed her every kindness which I had enjoyed, and she might have thought me ungrateful.

But I met in the fort with a last adventure, which I must not forget to relate.

On the following day, an officer dressed in the national uniform called upon the major, accompanied by an elderly man of about sixty years of age, wearing a sword, and, presenting to the major a dispatch with the seal of the war office, he waited for an answer, and went away as soon as he had received one from the governor.

After the officer had taken leave, the major, addressing himself to the elderly gentleman, to whom he gave the title of count, told him that his orders were to keep him a prisoner, and that he gave him the whole of the fort for his prison. The count offered him his sword, but the major nobly refused to take it, and escorted him to the room he was to occupy. Soon after, a servant in livery brought a bed and a trunk, and the next morning the same servant, knocking at my door, told me that his master begged the honour of my company to breakfast. I accepted the invitation, and he received me with these words:

"Dear sir, there has been so much talk in Venice about the skill with which you proved your incredible alibi, that I could not help asking for the honour of your acquaintance."

"But, count, the alibi being a true one, there can be no skill required to prove it. Allow me to say that those who doubt its truth are paying me a very poor compliment, for—"

"Never mind; do not let us talk any more of that, and forgive me. But as we happen to be companions in misfortune, I trust you will not refuse me your friendship. Now for breakfast."

After our meal, the count, who had heard from me some portion of my history, thought that my confidence called for a return on his part, and he began: "I am the Count de Bonafede. In my early days I served under Prince Eugene, but I gave up the army, and entered on a civil career in Austria. I had to fly from Austria and take refuge in Bavaria in consequence of an unfortunate duel. In Munich I made the acquaintance of a young lady belonging to a noble family; I eloped with her and brought her to Venice, where we were married. I have now been twenty years in Venice. I have six children, and everybody knows me. About a week ago I sent my servant to the postoffice for my letters, but they were refused him because he had not any money to pay the postage. I went myself, but the clerk would not deliver me my letters, although I assured him that I would pay for them the next time. This made me angry, and I called upon the Baron de Taxis, the postmaster, and complained of the clerk, but he answered very rudely that the clerk had simply obeyed his orders, and that my letters would only be delivered on payment of the postage. I felt very indignant, but as I was in his house I controlled my anger, went home, and wrote a note to him asking him to give me satisfaction for his rudeness, telling him that I would never go out without my sword, and that I would force him to fight whenever and wherever I should meet him. I never came across him, but yesterday I was accosted by the secretary of the inquisitors, who told me that I must forget the baron's rude conduct, and go under the guidance of an officer whom he pointed out to me, to imprison myself for a week in this fortress. I shall thus have the pleasure of spending that time with you."

I told him that I had been free for the last twenty-four hours, but that to shew my gratitude for his friendly confidence I would feel honoured if he would allow me to keep him company. As I had already engaged myself with the major, this was only a polite falsehood.

In the afternoon I happened to be with him on the tower of the fort, and pointed out a gondola advancing towards the lower gate; he took his spy-glass and told me that it was his wife and daughter coming to see him. We went to meet the ladies, one of whom might once have been worth the trouble of an elopement; the other, a young person between fourteen and sixteen, struck me as a beauty of a new style. Her hair was of a beautiful light auburn, her eyes were blue and very fine, her nose a Roman, and her pretty mouth, half-open and laughing, exposed a set of teeth as white as her complexion, although a beautiful rosy tint somewhat veiled the whiteness of the last. Her figure was so slight that it seemed out of nature, but her perfectly-formed breast appeared an altar on which the god of love would have delighted to breathe the sweetest incense. This splendid chest was, however, not yet well furnished, but in my imagination I gave her all the embonpoint which might have been desired, and I was so pleased that I could not take my looks from her. I met her eyes, and her laughing countenance seemed to say to me: "Only wait for two years, at the utmost, and all that your imagination is now creating will then exist in reality."

She was elegantly dressed in the prevalent fashion, with large hoops, and like the daughters of the nobility who have not yet attained the age of puberty, although the young countess was

217

marriageable. I had never dared to stare so openly at the bosom of a young lady of quality, but I thought there was no harm in fixing my eyes on a spot where there was nothing yet but in expectation.

The count, after having exchanged a few words in German with his wife, presented me in the most flattering manner, and I was received with great politeness. The major joined us, deeming it his duty to escort the countess all over the fortress, and I improved the excellent opportunity thrown in my way by the inferiority of my position; I offered my arm to the young lady, and the count left us to go to his room.

I was still an adept in the old Venetian fashion of attending upon ladies, and the young countess thought me rather awkward, though I believed myself very fashionable when I placed my hand under her arm, but she drew it back in high merriment. Her mother turned round to enquire what she was laughing at, and I was terribly confused when I heard her answer that I had tickled her.

"This is the way to offer your arm to a lady," she said, and she passed her hand through my arm, which I rounded in the most clumsy manner, feeling it a very difficult task to resume a dignified countenance. Thinking me a novice of the most innocent species, she very likely determined to make sport of me. She began by remarking that by rounding my arm as I had done I placed it too far from her waist, and that I was consequently out of drawing. I told her I did not know how to draw, and inquired whether it was one of her accomplishments.

"I am learning," she answered, "and when you call upon us I will shew you Adam and Eve, after the Chevalier Liberi; I have made a copy which has been found very fine by some professors, although they did not know it was my work."

"Why did you not tell them?"

"Because those two figures are too naked."

"I am not curious to see your Adam, but I will look at your Eve with pleasure, and keep your secret."

This answer made her laugh again, and again her mother turned round. I put on the look of a simpleton, for, seeing the advantage I could derive from her opinion of me, I had formed my plan at the very moment she tried to teach me how to offer my arm to a lady.

She was so convinced of my simplicity that she ventured to say that she considered her Adam by far more beautiful than her Eve, because in her drawing of the man she had omitted nothing, every muscle being visible, while there was none conspicuous in Eve. "It is," she added, "a figure with nothing in it."

"Yet it is the one which I shall like best."

"No; believe me, Adam will please you most."

This conversation had greatly excited me. I had on a pair of linen breeches, the weather being very warm.... I was afraid of the major and the countess, who were a few yards in front of us, turning round .... I was on thorns. To make matters worse, the young lady stumbled, one of her shoes slipped off, and presenting me her pretty foot she asked me to put the shoe right. I knelt on the ground, and, very likely without thinking, she lifted up her skirt.... she had very wide hoops and no petticoat.... what I saw was enough to strike me dead on the spot.... When I rose, she asked if anything was the matter with me.

A moment after, coming out of one of the casemates, her head-dress got slightly out of order, and she begged that I would remedy the accident, but, having to bend her head down, the state in which I was could no longer remain a secret for her. In order to avoid greater confusion to both of us, she enquired who had made my watch ribbon; I told her it was a present from my sister, and she desired to examine it, but when I answered her that it was fastened to the fob-pocket, and found that she disbelieved me, I added that she could see for herself. She put her hand to it, and a natural but involuntary excitement caused me to be very indiscreet. She must have felt vexed, for she saw that she had made a mistake in her estimate of my character; she became more timid, she would not laugh any more, and we joined her mother and the major who was shewing her, in a sentry-box, the body of Marshal de Schulenburg which had been deposited there until the mausoleum erected for him was completed. As for myself, I felt deeply ashamed. I thought myself the first man who had alarmed her innocence, and I felt ready to do anything to atone for the insult.

Such was my delicacy of feeling in those days. I used to credit people with exalted sentiments, which often existed only in my imagination. I must confess that time has entirely destroyed that delicacy; yet I do not believe myself worse than other men, my equals in age and inexperience.

We returned to the count's apartment, and the day passed off rather gloomily. Towards evening the ladies went away, but the countess gave me a pressing invitation to call upon them in Venice.

The young lady, whom I thought I had insulted, had made such a deep impression upon me that the seven following days seemed very long; yet I was impatient to see her again only that I might entreat her forgiveness, and convince her of my repentance.

The following day the count was visited by his son; he was plain-featured, but a thorough gentleman, and modest withal. Twenty-five years afterwards I met him in Spain, a cadet in the king's body-guard. He had served as a private twenty years before obtaining this poor promotion. The reader will hear of him in good time; I will only mention here that when I met him in Spain, he stood me out that I had never known him; his self-love prompted this very contemptible lie.

Early on the eighth day the count left the fortress, and I took my departure the same evening, having made an appointment at a coffee-house in St. Mark's Square with the major who was to accompany me to M. Grimani's house. I took leave of his wife, whose memory will always be dear to me, and she said, "I thank you for your skill in proving your alibi, but you have also to thank me for having understood you so well. My husband never heard anything about it until it was all over."

As soon as I reached Venice, I went to pay a visit to Madame Orio, where I was made welcome. I remained to supper, and my two charming sweethearts who were praying for the death of the bishop, gave me the most delightful hospitality for the night.

At noon the next day I met the major according to our appointment, and we called upon the Abbe Grimani. He received me with the air of a guilty man begging for mercy, and I was astounded at his stupidity when he entreated me to forgive Razetta and his companion. He told me that the bishop was expected very soon, and that he had ordered a room to be ready for me, and that I could take my meals with him. Then he introduced me to M. Valavero, a man of talent, who had just left the ministry of war, his term of office having lasted the usual six months. I paid my duty to him, and we kept up a kind of desultory conversation until the departure of the major. When he had left us M. Valavero entreated me to confess that I had been the guilty party in the attack upon Razetta. I candidly told him that the thrashing had been my handiwork, and I gave him all the particulars, which amused him immensely. He remarked that, as I had perpetrated the affair before midnight, the fools had made a mistake in their accusation; but that, after all, the mistake had not materially helped me in proving the alibi, because my sprained ankle, which everybody had supposed a real accident, would of itself have been sufficient.

But I trust that my kind reader has not forgotten that I had a very heavy weight upon my conscience, of which I longed to get rid. I had to see the goddess of my fancy, to obtain my pardon, or die at her feet.

I found the house without difficulty; the count was not at home. The countess received me very kindly, but her appearance caused me so great a surprise that I did not know what to say to her. I had fancied that I was going to visit an angel, that I would find her in a lovely paradise, and I found myself in a large sitting-room furnished with four rickety chairs and a dirty old table. There was hardly any light in the room because the shutters were nearly closed. It might have been a precaution against the heat, but I judged that it was more probably for the purpose of concealing the windows, the glass of which was all broken. But this visible darkness did not prevent me from remarking that the countess was wrapped up in an old tattered gown, and that her chemise did not shine by its cleanliness. Seeing that I was ill at ease, she left the room, saying that she would send her daughter, who, a few minutes afterwards, came in with an easy and noble appearance, and told me that she had expected me with great impatience, but that I had surprised her at a time at which she was not in the habit of receiving any visits.

I did not know what to answer, for she did not seem to me to be the same person. Her miserable dishabille made her look almost ugly, and I wondered at the impression she had produced upon me at the fortress. She saw my surprise, and partly guessed my thoughts, for she put on a look, not of vexation, but of sorrow which called forth all my pity. If she had been a philosopher she might have rightly despised me as a man whose sympathy was enlisted only by her fine dress, her nobility, or her apparent wealth; but she endeavoured to bring me round by her sincerity. She felt that if she could call a little sentiment into play, it would certainly plead in her favour.

"I see that you are astonished, reverend sir, and I know the reason of your surprise. You expected to see great splendour here, and you find only misery. The government allows my father but a small salary, and there are nine of us. As we must attend church on Sundays and holidays in a style proper to our condition, we are often compelled to go without our dinner, in order to get out of pledge the clothes which urgent need too often obliges us to part with, and which we pledge anew on the following day. If we did not attend mass, the curate would strike our names off the list of those who share the alms of the Confraternity of the Poor, and those alms alone keep us afloat."

What a sad tale! She had guessed rightly. I was touched, but rather with shame than true emotion. I was not rich myself, and, as I was no longer in love, I only heaved a deep sigh, and remained as cold as ice. Nevertheless, her position was painful, and I answered politely, speaking with kindness and assuring her of my sympathy. "Were I wealthy," I said, "I would soon shew you that your tale of woe has not fallen on unfeeling ears; but I am poor, and, being at the eve of my departure from Venice, even my friendship would be useless to you." Then, after some desultory talk, I expressed a hope that her beauty would yet win happiness for her. She seemed to consider for a few minutes, and said, "That may happen some day, provided that the man who feels the power of my charms understands that they can be bestowed only with my heart, and is willing to render me the justice I deserve; I am only looking for a lawful marriage, without dreaming of rank or fortune; I no longer believe in the first, and I know how to live without the second; for I have been accustomed to poverty, and even to abject need; but you cannot realize that. Come and see my drawings."

"You are very good, mademoiselle."

Alas! I was not thinking of her drawings, and I could no longer feel interested in her Eve, but I followed her.

We came to a chamber in which I saw a table, a chair, a small toilet-glass and a bed with the straw palliasse turned over, very likely for the purpose of allowing the looker-on to suppose that there were sheets underneath, but I was particularly disgusted by a certain smell, the cause of which was recent; I was thunderstruck, and if I had been still in love, this antidote would have been sufficiently powerful to cure me instanter. I wished for nothing but to make my escape, never to return, and I regretted that I could not throw on the table a handful of ducats, which I should have considered the price of my ransom.

The poor girl shewed me her drawings; they were fine, and I praised them, without alluding particularly to Eve, and without venturing a joke upon Adam. I asked her, for the sake of saying something, why she did not try to render her talent remunerative by learning pastel drawing.

"I wish I could," she answered, "but the box of chalks alone costs two sequins."

"Will you forgive me if I am bold enough to offer you six?"

"Alas! I accept them gratefully, and to be indebted to you for such a service makes me truly happy."

Unable to keep back her tears, she turned her head round to conceal them from me, and I took that opportunity of laying the money on the table, and out of politeness, wishing to spare her every unnecessary humiliation, I saluted her lips with a kiss which she was at liberty to consider a loving one, as I wanted her to ascribe my reserve to the respect I felt for her. I then left her with a promise to call another day to see her father. I never kept my promise. The reader will see how I met her again after ten years.

How many thoughts crowded upon my mind as I left that house! What a lesson! I compared reality with the imagination, and I had to give the preference to the last, as reality is always dependent on it. I then began to forsee a truth which has been clearly proved to me in my after life, namely, that love is only a feeling of curiosity more or less intense, grafted upon the inclination placed in us by nature that the species may be preserved. And truly, woman is like a book, which, good or bad, must at first please us by the frontispiece. If this is not interesting, we do not feel any wish to read the book, and our wish is in direct proportion to the interest we feel. The frontispiece of woman runs from top to bottom like that of a book, and her feet, which are most important to every man who shares my taste, offer the same interest as the edition of the work. If it is true that most amateurs bestow little or no attention upon the feet of a woman, it is likewise a fact that most readers care little or nothing whether a book is of the first edition or the tenth. At all events, women are quite right to take the greatest care of their face, of their dress, of their general appearance; for it is only by that part of the frontispiece that they can call forth a wish to read them in those men who have not been endowed by nature with the privilege of blindness. And just in the same manner that men, who have read a great many books, are certain to feel at last a desire for perusing new works even if they are bad, a man who has known many women, and all handsome women, feels at last a curiosity for ugly specimens when he meets with entirely new ones. It is all very well for his eye to discover the paint which conceals the reality, but his passion has become a vice, and suggests some argument in favour of the lying frontispiece. It is possible, at least he thinks so, that the work may prove better than the title-page, and the reality more acceptable than the paint which hides it. He then tries to peruse the book, but the leaves have not been opened; he meets with some resistance, the living book must be read according to established rules, and the book-worm falls a victim to a coquetry, the monster which persecutes all those who make a business of love. As for thee, intelligent man, who hast read the few preceding lines, let me tell thee that, if they do not assist in opening thy eyes, thou art lost; I mean that thou art certain of being a victim to the fair sex to the very last moment of thy life. If my candour does not displease thee, accept my congratulations. In the evening I called upon Madame Orio, as I wanted to inform her charming nieces that, being an inmate of Grimani's house, I could not sleep out for the first night. I found there the faithful Rosa, who told me that the affair of the alibi was in every mouth, and that, as such celebrity was evidently caused by a very decided belief in the untruth of the alibi itself, I ought to fear a retaliation of the same sort on the part of Razetta, and to keep on my guard, particularly at night. I felt all the importance of this advice, and I took care never to go out in the evening otherwise than in a gondola, or accompanied by some friends. Madame Manzoni told me that I was acting wisely, because, although the judges could not do otherwise than acquit me, everybody knew the real truth of the matter, and Razetta could not fail to be my deadly foe.

Three or four days afterwards M. Grimani announced the arrival of the bishop, who had put up at the convent of his order, at Saint-Francois de Paul. He presented me himself to the prelate as a jewel highly prized by himself, and as if he had been the only person worthy of descanting upon its beauty.

I saw a fine monk wearing his pectoral cross. He would have reminded me of Father Mancia if he had not looked stouter and less reserved. He was about thirty-four, and had been made a bishop by the grace of God, the Holy See, and my mother. After pronouncing over me a blessing, which I received kneeling, and giving me his hand to kiss, he embraced me warmly, calling me his dear son in the Latin language, in which he continued to address me. I thought that, being a Calabrian, he might feel ashamed of his Italian, but he undeceived me by speaking in that language to M. Grimani. He told me that, as he could not take me with him from Venice, I should have to proceed to Rome, where Grimani would take care to send me, and that I would procure his address at Ancona from one of his friends, called Lazari, a Minim monk, who would likewise supply me with the means of continuing my journey.

"When we meet in Rome," he added, "we can go together to Martorano by way of Naples. Call upon me to-morrow morning, and have your breakfast with me. I intend to leave the day after."

As we were on our way back to his house, M. Grimani treated me to a long lecture on morals, which nearly caused me to burst into loud laughter. Amongst other things, he informed me that I ought not to study too hard, because the air in Calabria was very heavy, and I might become consumptive from too close application to my books.

The next morning at day-break I went to the bishop. After saying his mass, we took some chocolate, and for three hours he laid me under examination. I saw clearly that he was not pleased with me, but I was well enough pleased with him. He seemed to me a worthy man, and as he was to lead me along the great highway of the Church, I felt attracted towards him, for, at the time, although I entertained a good opinion of my personal appearance, I had no confidence whatever in my talents.

After the departure of the good bishop, M. Grimani gave me a letter left by him, which I was to deliver to Father Lazari, at the Convent of the Minims, in Ancona. M. Grimani informed me that he would send me to that city with the ambassador from Venice, who was on the point of sailing. I had therefore to keep myself in readiness, and, as I was anxious to be out of his hands, I approved all his arrangements. As soon as I had notice of the day on which the suite of the ambassador would embark, I went to pay my last farewell to all my acquaintances. I left my brother Francois in the school of M. Joli, a celebrated decorative painter. As the peotta in which I was to sail would not leave before daybreak, I spent the short night in the arms of the two sisters, who, this time, entertained no hope of ever seeing me again. On my side I could not forsee what would happen, for I was abandoning myself to fate, and I thought it would be useless to think of the future. The night was therefore spent between joy and sadness, between pleasures and tears. As I bade them adieu, I returned the key which had opened so often for me the road to happiness.

This, my first love affair, did not give me any experience of the world, for our intercourse was always a happy one, and was never disturbed by any quarrel or stained by any interested motive. We often felt, all three of us, as if we must raise our souls towards the eternal Providence of God, to thank Him for having, by His particular protection, kept from us all the accidents which might have disturbed the sweet peace we were enjoying.

I left in the hands of Madame Manzoni all my papers, and all the forbidden books I possessed. The good woman, who was twenty years older than I, and who, believing in an immutable destiny, took pleasure in turning the leaves of the great book of fate, told me that she was certain of restoring to me all I left with her, before the end of the following year, at the latest. Her prediction caused me both surprise and pleasure, and feeling deep reverence for her, I thought myself bound to assist the realization of her foresight. After all, if she predicted the future, it was not through superstition, or in consequence of some vain foreboding which reason must condemn, but through her knowledge of the world, and of the nature of the person she was addressing. She used to laugh because she never made a mistake.

I embarked from St. Mark's landing. M. Grimani had given me ten sequins, which he thought would keep me during my stay in the lazzaretto of Ancona for the necessary quarantine, after which it was not to be supposed that I could want any money. I shared Grimani's certainty on the subject, and with my natural thoughtlessness I cared nothing about it. Yet I must say that, unknown to everybody, I had in my purse forty bright sequins, which powerfully contributed to increase my cheerfulness, and I left Venice full of joy and without one regret.

The End